SYRACUSE 415–413 BC

Destruction of the Athenian Imperial Fleet

CAMPAIGN • 195

SYRACUSE 415–413 BC

Destruction of the Athenian Imperial Fleet

NIC FIELDS

ILLUSTRATED BY PETER DENNIS

Series editors Marcus Cowper and Nikolai Bogdanovic

First published in Great Britain in 2008 by Osprey Publishing
Midland House, West Way, Botley, Oxford OX2 0PH, UK
443 Park Avenue South, New York, NY 10016, USA
E-mail: info@ospreypublishing.com

A CIP catalogue record for this book is available from the British Library.

ISBN 978 1 84603 258 5

Editorial: Ilios Publishing, Oxford, UK (www.iliospublishing.com)
Design: The Black Spot
Cartography: The Map Studio
Bird's-eye view artworks: The Black Spot
Index by Alison Worthington
Typeset in Sabon and Myriad Pro
Originated by United Graphic Pte Ltd., Singapore
Printed in China through Worldprint

08 09 10 11 12   10 9 8 7 6 5 4 3 2 1

FOR A CATALOGUE OF ALL BOOKS PUBLISHED BY OSPREY MILITARY
AND AVIATION PLEASE CONTACT:

NORTH AMERICA
Osprey Direct, c/o Random House Distribution Center, 400 Hahn Road,
Westminster, MD 21157
E-mail: info@ospreydirect.com

ALL OTHER REGIONS
Osprey Direct UK, P.O. Box 140 Wellingborough, Northants, NN8 2FA, UK
E-mail: info@ospreydirect.co.uk

www.ospreypublishing.com

THE WOODLAND TRUST

Osprey Publishing are supporting the Woodland Trust, the UK's leading woodland conservation charity, by funding the dedication of trees.

ABBREVIATIONS

Fornara	C.W. Fornara, *Translated Documents of Greece and Rome I: Archaic Times to the end of the Peloponnesian War*[2] (Cambridge 1983)
IG	*Inscriptiones Graecae* (Berlin 1923–)

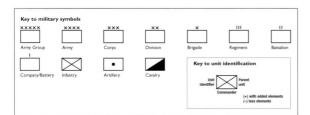

Key to military symbols — Army Group, Army, Corps, Division, Brigade, Regiment, Battalion, Company/Battery, Infantry, Artillery, Cavalry. Key to unit identification: Unit identifier / Parent unit / Commander; (+) with added elements, (−) less elements.

ARTIST'S NOTE

Readers may care to note that the original paintings from which the colour plates in this book were prepared are available for private sale. The Publishers retain all reproduction copyright whatsoever. All enquiries should be addressed to:

Peter Dennis, Fieldhead,
The Park, Mansfield,
Nottinghamshire
NG18 2AT,
UK

GLOSSARY

Antilabê	Handgrip of *aspis* (q.v.).
Aspis	'Argive shield', a soup-bowl-shaped shield, some 80 to 100cm in diameter, held via an *antilabê* (q.v.) and a *porpax* (q.v.).
Boulê	In Athens the council of Five Hundred, 50 from each tribe, which prepared the business for the *ekklêsia* (q.v.), provided its president, and saw that its decisions were carried out.
Dêmos	The common people, the most numerous body of citizens of the *polis* (q.v.), though in democratic Athens the word also stood for the sovereign citizen body as a whole.
Doru	'Dorian spear', a thrusting spear, 2 to 2.5m in length, armed with a spearhead (bronze or iron) and a *saurotêr* (q.v.).
Ekklêsia	In Athens the sovereign political body, open to all male citizens aged 18 and over.
Epibatês/ epibatai	'Deck-soldier', hoplite (q.v.) serving as a marine on a trireme.
Helots	Indentured serfs who worked the land of Spartans and served as attendants and lightly armed troops in war.
Hoplite	Heavily-armed foot soldier accustomed to fighting shoulder-to-shoulder in a phalanx.
Knemides	Greaves, bronze armour for the lower legs.
Kopis	Single-edged, heavy, slashing-type sword shaped like a machete, the hoplite's secondary weapon.
Linothôrax	Stiff linen corselet, which is lighter and more flexible (but more expensive) than bronze body armour.
Mantis/ manteis	Seer.
Metoikos/ metoikoi	Non-citizen inhabitant of Athens – could not own land but was liable to special taxes and military service.
Neodamôdes/ neodamôdeis	Newly enfranchised helot (q.v.).
Ôthismos	Pushing stage of hoplite battle.
Paean	Collective war cry sung in unison, Dorian in origin but eventually adopted by other Greeks.
Panopliâ	'Full armour', the panoply of a hoplite (q.v.).
Polis/poleis	Conventionally translated as 'city-state', the term actually refers to an autonomous political community of Greeks.
Porpax	Armband of *aspis* (q.v.).
Pteruges	'Feathers', stiffened leather or linen fringing on *linothôrax* (q.v.).
Saurotêr	Bronze butt-spike.
Stratêgos/ stratêgoi	General.
Talent	Fixed weight of silver equivalent to 60 *minae* (Attic-Euboic *tálanton* = 26.2kg, Aiginetan *tálanton* = 43.6kg).

CONTENTS

The allies of Athens and Syracuse at the time of the fourth and final sea battle in the Great Harbour (after Thucydides, 7.57)

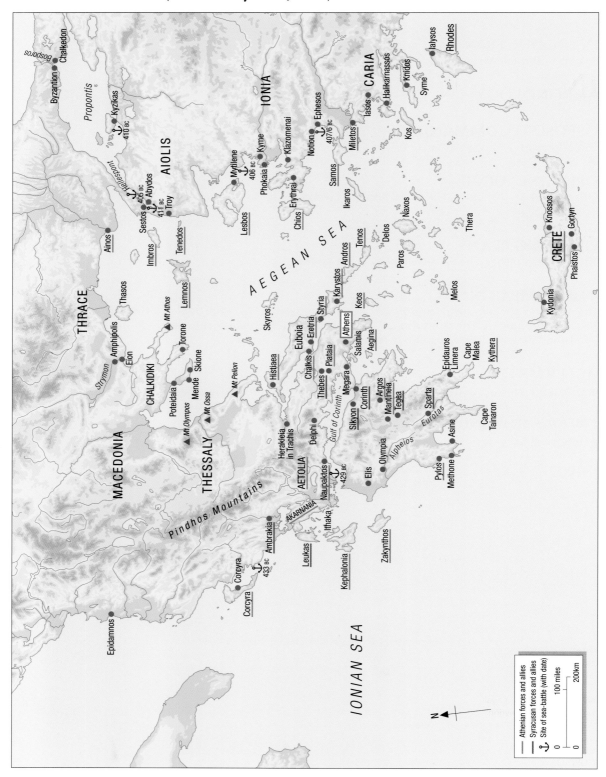

INTRODUCTION

Shortly after the midsummer of 415 BC, Athens launched a long-distance strike on Syracuse, the principal Greek state of the rich grain-producing island of Sicily and a potential ally of Sparta. The claim by Alcibiades, the brilliant but reckless Athenian general, was that the Syracusans were providing valuable foodstuffs to the Spartans and their allies. Moreover, his argument went, if Athens could establish itself in Sicily then it would be in a commanding position for future aggrandisement against Carthage. Possession of Syracuse would allow the Athenians to dominate the western Mediterranean. Likewise, the conquest of Syracuse promised rich booty and additional imperial revenues. Alcibiades' dazzling oratory won over the citizens to his grandiose plan, overturning the more cautious suggestions of his political rival Nikias. Caring little that Syracuse was over 900km distant, had ample financial reserves, good cavalry and a sizeable navy, the Athenians eagerly voted to attack.

The Athenian historian Thucydides,[1] whose contemporary account is a literary masterpiece, provides an ambivalent assessment of the enterprise, emphasizing the foolhardy ambition so typical of imperial democracy, and yet,

1 Throughout, references are to Thucydides' *History of the Peloponnesian War* unless otherwise indicated. Thus the numbers refer to the traditional division by book, chapter and verse only, unless confusion might result, in which case the abbreviation 'Thucydides' is used.

Ortygia, looking north-north-east from the harbour entrance. 'Stretched in front of a Syracusan bay lies an island', narrates Aeneas, 'over against wave-beaten Plemmyrion' (Virgil *Aeneid* 3.692–93). Named the inner city, the island was the fortified centre of Syracuse. (Fields-Carré Collection)

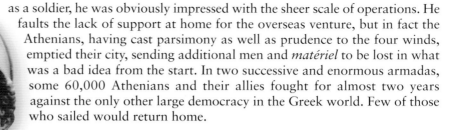

as a soldier, he was obviously impressed with the sheer scale of operations. He faults the lack of support at home for the overseas venture, but in fact the Athenians, having cast parsimony as well as prudence to the four winds, emptied their city, sending additional men and *matériel* to be lost in what was a bad idea from the start. In two successive and enormous armadas, some 60,000 Athenians and their allies fought for almost two years against the only other large democracy in the Greek world. Few of those who sailed would return home.

ORIGINS OF THE CAMPAIGN

After the defeat of the Persians at Salamis (480 BC) and Plataia (479 BC), Athens rose to become the top city-state (*polis*) in the Greek world. As the leading maritime power it made itself the strongest member of what modern commentators call the Delian League, an alliance of Greek city-states (*poleis*) dedicated to continuing the war of liberation and vengeance against Persia. To the common effort the members of this league contributed ships plus crews or, if more agreeable to them, money, which was kept in the shrine of Apollo on the sacred island of Delos.

Under Themistokles and a succession of gifted imperialists, the alliance grew rapidly through a mixture of voluntary adherence and a use of force until it embraced nearly all the *poleis* of the islands and coasts of the Aegean. The studied Athenian policy was to encourage those members who contributed ships to substitute a monetary payment, until only Lesbos, Samos, and Chios were left with a navy and enjoyed relative autonomy. First its leader, then its master, Athens gradually attained a position where it could demand virtually any dues to the league and did not have to account for the money sent to the league treasury. No longer used solely for common defence, the Athenians spent much of what was now, in effect, imperial tribute – 600 talents a year out of total revenue of 1,000 – turning their city into a cultural and architectural showpiece, which made those independent-minded Greek allies contributing the money more and more resentful.

As a 'benign' police force of sorts for its tribute-paying allies, Athenian triremes enforced as well as expanded Athens' dominion over as much of the Aegean as possible, creating satellite democracies in the process. At its apogee the Athenian maritime empire ruled directly or indirectly some 150 *poleis*, the most remote of these being a mere eight-day voyage or 400km from the Peiraieus, the port of Athens, while Athenian power could be projected over the Mediterranean from Sicily to Egypt to the Black Sea. In time, a number of anxious *poleis* looked to oligarchic Sparta for leadership. In their eyes the Athenians were not Perikles' 'standard-bearers of civilization', who had developed political equality, perfected drama, built the Parthenon, and fashioned a dynamic culture based on expropriated capital, but rather an oppressive and unpredictable imperialist state, whose navy and democracy ensured turmoil for any who chose to stand in its way. Like all such myths, this particular myth of 'Periklean Athens' is true in parts. However, like all superpowers since, Athens saw no contradiction between democratic freedom at home and aggressive imperialism overseas. The causes of what is conventionally called the Peloponnesian War (431–404 BC) may be controversial, but there is no good reason to doubt Thucydides' view that the fundamental cause was Sparta's fear of Athenian imperialism.

Marble bust of Perikles (London, British Museum, GR 1805.7-3.91), a 2nd-century Roman copy from Hadrian's Villa, Tivoli. It was under Perikles that Athens would become a cultural showpiece. It also became the greatest maritime empire that the Mediterranean had ever known. (Fields-Carré Collection)

Thucydides on war

Today, as much as any other time, the causes of war are controversial subjects. We must, therefore, be very wary of reasons why certain ancient conflicts took place. By the classical period wars were no longer fought for so-called living space as in the Lelantine War (*c.* 734–680 BC) or the First Messenian War (*c.* 730–710 BC). There are no examples of the victor seizing territory from the vanquished, only examples of tribute exacted or garrisons planted. Secondly, wars were not fought in this period for reasons of economics. In Athens, for instance, trade and industry was firmly in the hands of the *metoikoi*, the resident foreigners, who by definition had no say in Athenian affairs.

If there was a single cause it was *holos*, a state seeking to gain hegemony (*hêgemonia*), whereby the autonomy of one power can be secured through the subjugation of others, or those others preventing it. The Old Oligarch, an anonymous figure who wrote a ranting political pamphlet on Athens while Thucydides was collecting material for his history, promoted the advantages of hegemony, that is, the Athenian empire, because it provided tangible results for Athens (Pseudo-Xenophon *Athenaiôn politeia* 2.2–8, 11–14). However, such material things were not as important as the intangible feeling of power, an imperial perspective fully appreciated by Alcibiades: 'It is not possible for us to calculate, like housekeepers, exactly how much empire we want to have' (6.18.3). Alcibiades' argument that an imperial power cannot be inactive would be one recognized by any modern superpower.

Naturally, hegemony created in other people the desire to be protected from the likes of Athens. Many Greeks, quite rightly, wanted to run their own affairs, no matter how sanguinary, without outside interference. Despite Perikles' boast that Athens was 'an education to Greece' (2.41.1), most Greek states were just as sophisticated and as advanced in cultural and political affairs as it was. Besides, what right did the Athenians have rowing around the Aegean peddling their radical democracy, a socio-political heresy to most Greeks?

The fortification walls of Poteidaia. A Corinthian colony on the isthmus of Pallene, Thrace, Poteidaia had been 'incorporated' into the Athenian empire. In 432 BC Athens demanded that the Poteidaians dismiss their Corinthian magistrates and dismantle their walls, so prompting their rebellion. (Fields-Carré Collection)

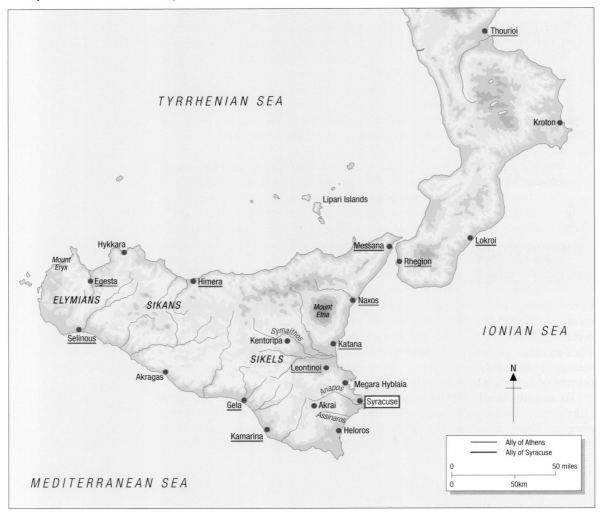

Thucydides (1.23–65) provides what is now considered a celebrated analysis on the origin of the great conflict between Athens and Sparta. He starts by distinguishing between the true cause of the war from what he calls the 'causes of complaint' and the 'specific instances where their interests clashed' (1.23.5). The distinctions made by him are not so much between fundamental causes for the war but primarily ones between the 'real reason', which was 'least talked about' (1.23.6), that is to say, in the speeches of the various envoys, and the 'accusations', which were openly expressed by both sides. In Thucydides' view, the so-called accusations pivoted upon Corcyra's appeal to Athens (1.31–55) and Poteidaia's revolt from Athenian control (1.56–65).

However, for Thucydides what made the war between Athens and Sparta inevitable was Sparta's fear of the growing power of Athens. Yet this 'real reason' was least discussed because Sparta could hardly stand before the members of its alliance, what is often called nowadays the Peloponnesian League, and pronounce that it was afraid of Athens. Notwithstanding Sparta's candid behaviour, Thucydides resolutely believes that fear of Athens was the root cause of the war. For instance, he records the envoys from

Corcyra (Corfu) warning the Athenians that 'Sparta is frightened of you and wants war' (1.33.3). Again, he says the Spartans thought that war should be declared 'not so much because they were influenced by the speeches of their allies as because they were afraid of the further growth of Athenian power, seeing, as they did, that already the greater part of Hellas was under the control of Athens' (1.88).

To amplify this last point Thucydides gives his famous *Pentekontaetia* (1.89–117), the 50-year excursus that charts the growth of Athenian power after the defeat of the Persians. That accomplished, Thucydides then presents the final and most definite statement as to why the Spartans, though they saw what was happening, 'did little or nothing to prevent the growth of Athenian power, and for most of the time remained inactive, being traditionally slow to go to war, unless they were forced to' (1.118.2). In Thucydides' eyes, therefore, the Spartans were not warmongers. Theirs was a traditional society, proud of its ways and conscious of its prestige: the Athenians – innovative, cocksure and greedy – represented everything they distrusted. However, when Athens started to meddle with Sparta's allies, namely Corinth and the antagonism that arose between the Athenians and the Corinthians over the control of Corcyra (433 BC) and Poteidaia (432 BC), the Spartans were left with little choice. This was especially so when another important ally, Megara, added its voice to the clamour for war.

The Peloponnesian War

Now able to invade Attica (Athens' home territory) through the Megarid (the stretch of land between the Corinthian and Saronic gulfs under Megarian control), Sparta did so on five occasions during the initial phase of the war (431 BC, 430 BC, 428 BC, 427 BC, and 425 BC). The land invasion of 446 BC and its dramatic success in bringing the so-called First Peloponnesian War to a swift end had convinced the Spartans and their allies (known collectively as the Peloponnesians) that a similar strategy would bring about the same result. Yet the Spartans (but not King Archidamos) had failed to realize that Perikles and the Athenians were planning a totally new strategy.

The north gateway (Syracuse Gate) at Heloros. This was not in fact a true *polis*, but a Syracusan colony established to guarantee the integrity of its territory and to guard against threats either from other Greeks or from the Sikels. (Fields-Carré Collection)

On Perikles' advice, the Athenians took refuge inside the fortification walls surrounding Athens and the Peiraieus, abandoning the countryside to the Peloponnesian incursions and relying on the sea routes to supply the city with grain from the Black Sea region. The Athenians responded to the Spartan ravaging merely by minor cavalry operations, sea-borne raids on the Peloponnese, and an annual devastation of the Megarid after the Peloponnesians had returned home after their invasion of Attica. Thus by avoiding pitched battles, the Athenians limited the effectiveness of Sparta's main military strength. But after Perikles' death (429 BC), Athens, now dominated by the demagogue Kleon, adopted a more daring, offensive strategy. Not only did it establish bases on the Peloponnesian coast – notably at Pylos in Messenia – it also attempted to knock Boiotia out of the war, the second invasion ending in a thundering defeat at Delion (424 BC).

The same year saw the Spartan Brasidas surprising Athens with a campaign in the Thraceward region, winning over a number of Athens' dependencies, including Amphipolis. What Brasidas realized was Sparta's need to open up a second front to destabilize Athens' alliance from within. Already two years previously the Spartans had planted a military colony in central Greece, Herakleia in Trachis, which not only put pressure on Athens' control of Euboia but also lay en route to its allies in the far north, Amphipolis chief among them. His own death, and that of Kleon, in battle outside the city (422 BC), led to the signing of a peace treaty. Amphipolis, however, never returned to the Athenian fold.

The Peace of Nikias, or 'hollow peace' as Thucydides (5.26.2) so aptly calls it, was soon in tatters when an increasing number of Athenians turned their thoughts to a more aggressive policy. Their spokesman was the ambitious Alcibiades, who cobbled together what was an anti-Spartan league in the Peloponnese and took Athens back to war. Yet this came to nought when the Spartans destroyed the coalition forces, led by Athens and Argos, at Mantineia (418 BC).

Again at Alcibiades' urging, Athens opened a whole new front by launching an expedition against Syracuse (415 BC), with Alcibiades himself, along with his political rival Nikias, as one of its three commanders. Before the attack on Syracuse itself had begun, however, Alcibiades was recalled home to answer charges of sacrilege. He made his way to Sparta and then proceeded to make himself indispensable by terrifying the Spartans with an account of Athenian plans for total conquest of the far west. Meanwhile, while Alcibiades dallied in Sparta, the Athenians got bogged down outside Syracuse and the expedition ended in horror.

CHRONOLOGY

479–465 BC   **Emergence of imperial Athens**

479/478 BC   Foundation of Delian League (anti-Persian).

478 BC   City walls of Athens begun; Athenian expeditions to Byzantion, Sestos and Cyprus; Sparta quits Delian League.

476/475 BC   Athenian expeditions to Eïon and Skyros (bones of 'Theseus' saga).

474 BC   Hieron of Syracuse defeats Etruscans at Kyme.

c. 473 BC   Aristides coerces Karystos to join Delian League.

c. 472 BC   Aischylos' *Persai*.

c. 471 BC   Themistokles ostracized (flees to Persia).

c. 470 BC   Naxos quits Delian League.

469 BC   Accession of King Archidamos of Sparta.

467 BC   Fall of the Deinomenid tyranny in Syracuse (establishment of democracy).

c. 466 BC   Kimon's victory over Persian fleet on the Eurymedon.

465 BC   Thasos quits Delian League.

c. 464–460 BC   **Sparta's domestic problems (war with Tegea, Mantineia goes democratic, Fourth Messenian War).**

461 BC   Kimon ostracized (pro-Spartan); Ephialtes' radical democratic reforms (assassinated); emergence of Perikles as pre-eminent political and military leader.

461/460 BC   Athenian alliance with Argos, Thessaly and Megara.

460–440 BC   **First Peloponnesian War**

460/459 BC   Athenian expedition to Egypt.

c. 458 BC   Long Walls of Athens begun.

458 BC   Saronic Gulf conflict (siege of Aegina); Athenian victories in Megarid.

458/457 BC   Battles of Tanagra and Oenophyta (Athens controls Boiotia); Athenian alliance with Egesta.

456 BC   Tolmides' sea-borne raid round Peloponnese.

c. 455 BC   Birth of Thucydides.

454 BC   Disaster for Athens in Nile Delta.

454/453 BC   Delian League treasury transferred from Delos to Athens (metamorphosis of league to empire complete).

453 BC   Erythrai and Miletos revolt from Athens; first extant Athenian Tribute List.

452/451 BC   Return of Kimon.

451 BC   Five-year truce between Athens and Sparta; Kimon campaigns (and dies) on Cyprus.

451/450 BC   Perikles' citizenship law (limited to those who were of Athenian birth on both sides); first Athenian citizen-colonies (*klêrouchies*).

449/448 BC   Peace of Kallias (détente between Athens and Persia).

447 BC	Perikles' building programme begun (Parthenon).
447/446 BC	Boiotia and Euboia revolt from Athens; battle of Koroneia (ends Athens' control of Boiotia); secession of Megara.
446 BC	Peloponnesian invasion of Attica; Perikles quashes Euboian revolt.
446/445 BC	Thirty Years Peace (Greek world split into two power blocs).
444/443 BC	Athens sponsors pan-Hellenic colony (*apoikia*) at Thourioi; Athenian alliances with Leontinoi and Rhegion.
440 BC	Samos revolts from Athens.

440–432 BC Between the wars

439 BC	Samos surrenders.
438 BC	Dedication of Parthenon.
437 BC	Propylaea begun.
437/436 BC	Athens establishes citizen-colony (*klêrouchia*) at Amphipolis.
c. 435 BC	Perikles' Black Sea expedition.
434 BC	Corcyra and Corinth clash.
433 BC	Athenian alliance with Corcyra (Corinth and Athens quarrel over Corcyra); battle of Sybota.
433/432 BC	Athenian alliances with Leontinoi and Rhegion renewed.
432 BC	Poteidaia revolts from Athens (Corinth and Athens quarrel over Poteidaia); conferences at Sparta and ultimatum to Athens (Sparta's fear of Athens, i.e. Thucydides' 'real reason').

431–421 BC Peloponnesian War (Archidamian War)

431 BC	Thebes attacks Plataia; first Peloponnesian land invasion of Attica; first Athenian sea-borne raid round Peloponnese; Athenians ravage Megarid; Perikles' 'Funeral Speech'.
430 BC	Second Peloponnesian land invasion of Attica; outbreak of plague in Athens; Poteidaia surrenders to Athenians.

429 BC	Peloponnesians besiege Plataia; Phormio's victories in Corinthian Gulf; death of Perikles; Sophokles' *Oedipus Tyrannus*.
c. 428 BC	Birth of Xenophon.
428 BC	Third Peloponnesian land invasion of Attica; Mytilene revolts from Athens.
c. 427 BC	Birth of Plato.
427 BC	Fourth Peloponnesian land invasion of Attica; Mytilene surrenders to Athenians; Nikias captures Minoa; Plataia surrenders to Peloponnesians; death of Archidamos; civil war (*stasis*) in Corcyra; first Athenian military intervention in Sicily; plague returns to Athens; rhetorician and sophist Gorgias of Leontinoi visits Athens.
426 BC	Sparta sends colony (*apoikia*) to Herakleia in Trachis; Demosthenes' Aetolian campaign; battle of Olpai.
425 BC	Ascendancy of demagogue Kleon; fifth Peloponnesian land invasion of Attica; Athenian reinforcements sent to Sicily; Pylos campaign (capture of 120 Spartiates); Aristophanes' *Acharnians*.
424 BC	Athenians capture Kythera, Nisaia and Megara's Long Walls; peace in Sicily (Athenians withdraw); Brasidas captures Amphipolis (Thucydides exiled); battle of Delion; Aristophanes' *Knights*.
423 BC	One-year armistice begins; succession of Dareios II Ochos; Skione and Mende revolt from Athens; Athenians recover Mende and besiege Skione; Euripides' *Suppliants*.
422 BC	Expiry of armistice; battle of Amphipolis (Brasidas and Kleon killed).
421 BC	Peace of Nikias (Thucydides' 'hollow peace'); Aristophanes' *Peace*.

421–413 BC Peloponnesian War ('hollow peace')

421/420 BC	Temple of Athena Nike erected.
420 BC	Alcibiades' quadruple alliance between Athens, Argos, Mantineia and Elis.
418 BC	Battle of Mantineia (opportunity to defeat Sparta on land squandered); alliance between Sparta and Argos.

416 BC	Athenians besiege and sack Melos (Thucydides' Melian Dialogue); Egestaian embassy to Athens.
415 BC	Spring: Euripides' *Trojan Women*; Athenians vote to launch expedition to Sicily.
	Summer: profanation of Eleusian Mysteries and mutilation of Herms; Athenian expedition to Sicily sets sail.
	Autumn: recall of Alcibiades (first downfall); Athenians take Hykkara; battle of the Anapos.
	Winter: Hermokrates calls for army reforms; Syracusans extend city walls ('winter wall'); Alcibiades in Sparta.
414 BC	Spring: Aristophanes' *Birds*; Spartans vote to send Gylippos to Syracuse; Athenians invest Syracuse; Lamachos killed (Nikias in sole command); Hermokrates dismissed.
	Summer: Aristophanes' *Amphiaraos*; Gylippos arrives at Syracuse; third Syracusan counter-wall; Nikias fortifies Plemmyrion.
	Autumn: Syracusans start naval training; Nikias' letter to Athenians.
	Winter: Athenians decide to send second expedition.
413 BC	Spring: Peloponnesians fortify Dekeleia; first sea-battle in Great Harbour (loss of Plemmyrion); second sea-battle in Great Harbour (Athenians defeated).
	Summer: second expedition under Demosthenes arrives; failure of night attack on Epipolai; lunar eclipse; third sea-battle in Great Harbour (Eurymedon killed); fourth and final sea-battle in Great Harbour.
	Autumn: retreat and destruction of Athenian army; Nikias and Demosthenes executed; subject allies of Athens begin to revolt.

413–404 BC Peloponnesian War (Ionian War)

412 BC	Spartan alliance with Persia (gold floats sizeable Peloponnesian fleet) and intervention in Aegean; revolts of Chios, Klazomenai and Miletos.

411 BC	Four Hundred rule Athens (democracy overthrown); revolt of Euboia; Athenian fleet at Samos remains loyal to democracy (Alcibiades takes command); battles of Kynossema and Abydos.
410 BC	Battle of Kyzikos; full democracy restored in Athens; temple of Athena Nike receives new parapet ('Wingless Nike').
409 BC	Spartans capture Chios; Carthaginians invade Sicily and take Selinous; Syracusans withdraw triremes from Aegean.
409/408 BC	Spartans retake Pylos.
408 BC	Athenians recover Chalkedon and Byzantion; Carthaginians sack Himera and return to Carthage.
408/407 BC	Failed *coup d'état* of Hermokrates in Syracuse.
407 BC	Alcibiades returns to Athens; Cyrus, prince of Persia, super-satrap of western Anatolia; Lysandros admiral (*nauarchos*).
407/406 BC	Battle of Notion; Alcibiades deposed (second downfall)
406 BC	Carthaginians return to Sicily and sack Akragas; battle of Arginousai (execution of Athenian *stratêgoi*); Lysandros restored to command; deaths of Euripides and Sophokles.
405 BC	Dionysios *stratêgos autokrator* of Syracuse; Carthaginians sack Gela and Kamarina; Carthaginians besiege Syracuse (camp struck by plague); treaty between Dionysios and Carthage; accession of Artaxerxes II Mnemon; battle of Aigospotamoi; Athens blockaded; Aristophanes' *Frogs*.
404 BC	Alcibiades assassinated; Athens defeated.

OPPOSING COMMANDERS

The conditions of ancient warfare placed practical limits on the powers of generals (*stratêgoi*). A conventional classical Greek battle was fought without reserves, and there was the essentially democratic expectation that a general (*stratêgos*) should lead from the front. This meant in the thick of an engagement he could do little about directing its course. Once a *stratêgos* had deployed his hoplites and battle had been joined, there was little or no room for command or manoeuvre, the individual *stratêgos* taking up his position in the front rank of the phalanx and fighting alongside his men. Consequently, many *stratêgoi* perished in the fray. It was outward displays of grit, not strategic or tactical skills, which were all important for a *stratêgos*.

THE ATHENIANS

The democratic system of Athens was a vigorous institution. The main decision-making body was the assembly, the *ekklêsia*, which all adult males of Athenian birth on both sides and over 18 were eligible to attend. To help the assembly with its deliberations, there was an annually elected council of 500 citizens over the age of 30, the *boulê*, which would prepare an agenda for the assembly. The vast majority of the executive officials who carried out the will of the Athenian people, the *dêmos*, were not elected but annually selected by lot, and could not hold the same office twice. Once in office, the people retained a tight control upon their magistrates, as manifest by the narrow job descriptions and the fact that they were scrutinized before, during and after their term of office.

Yet the Athenians were level-headed enough to realize that the people as a whole could not govern the state. Hence the top officials in Athens, the ten *stratêgoi*, were unique by virtue of the fact that the candidates, invariably well-to-do if not of 'good birth', were elected annually by the assembly from citizens aged over 30 (Anon. *Athenaiôn politeia* 61.1). However, unlike other magistrates, *stratêgoi* could be re-elected as long as they held the confidence of the electorate, and in this way they might exercise great personal influence and ensure an all-important continuity of policy. Perikles, for instance, is recorded as having been elected 15 times in succession (443/2–429/8 BC). While this office was his constitutional base, his practical political effectiveness came from his forceful personality, his persuasiveness, his admitted foresight, his strategic talent, his recognized integrity, and the general respect he commanded. Indeed, so great was his authority that Thucydides famously declared that this meant that 'in what was nominally a democracy, power was really in the hands of the first citizen' (2.65.9).

The south gateway (Syracuse Gate) at Leontinoi. The *polis* had entered into an alliance with Athens in an attempt to break free of Syracusan political domination. However, after the Athenians withdrew in 424 BC Leontinoi was quickly overrun by Syracuse. (Fields-Carré Collection)

As a natural consequence, therefore, the position of *stratêgos* quite quickly became the principal political prize for an ambitious Athenian. Such elections, as Aristotle (*Politics* 1273a 26–27) points out, were undemocratic as they allowed for birth, wealth and ability to be taken into account. Yet without direct elections one feels that any fool could have cropped up and led Athens, especially in wartime. Even an ultra-democrat would have been loath to entrust Athenian fortunes in battle to whomsoever the lottery happened to throw up. An army of sheep led by a lion would defeat an army of lions led by a sheep, or so says an Arab proverb.

Ultimately, every magistrate, whether directly elected or selected randomly by lot, was kept in check by the Athenian people. Even the 'blue-blooded' Perikles, during his penultimate year as a *stratêgos,* was stripped of his command and fined the enormous sum of 15 talents when the assembly decided to blame him for the plague. Yet this was mild compared with the 20-year exile of Thucydides or the dreadful fate of the six *stratêgoi* after Arginousai, a battle they had won for the fickle democratic assembly.

'I congratulate the Athenians', says Philip of Macedon sardonically, 'for finding ten *stratêgoi* every year; I have only ever found one, Parmenio' (Plutarch *Moralia* 177C). Yet the incumbent required a whole range of skills as the position itself took on executive duties that were more than merely military in nature. As such, the responsibilities of the *stratêgoi* were those of domestic and foreign policy subject to the control of the assembly. Fortifications and munitions, both military and naval armaments, mustering of citizen-soldiers and oarsmen and the imposition of war taxes all fell within the scope of their administration.

Though they were more than military commanders Athenian *stratêgoi* could of course be appointed as commanders both in the field and at sea, taking responsibility for strategic and – up to a point – tactical decisions. However, as already alluded to, the conditions of Greek warfare placed practical limits on the nature of command exercised by a *stratêgos*, Athenian and non-Athenian alike. Still, in his details concerning the preliminaries to the first Sicilian expedition, Thucydides says the Athenians 'selected as *stratêgoi*

with special powers (*autokratores*) for the expedition Alcibiades, the son of Kleinias, Nikias, the son of Nikeratos, and Lamachos, the son of Xenophanes' (6.8.2). In this case it was clearly the distance and difficulty of communications that entailed this extraordinary grant to allow them to make decisions on the spot, without referring back to Athens. Yet they could be called to account for their actions, and, as we shall discover, ultimate authority resided in the Athenian assembly. Alcibiades was the youngest of the three – he was not yet 40 – but he belonged to one of the most distinguished families of Athens, the Alkmaionidai and was thereby related to Perikles. He had first been elected *stratêgos* only four years previously. Nikias and Lamachos were older, more experienced men.

Nikias (d. 413 BC)

Though a non-aristocrat – his family cannot be traced back beyond his father Nikeratos – Nikias was certainly well-to-do. Nikeratos had created the family fortune by the exploitation of mining interest, so much so that his son was comfortable enough to be able to hire out 1,000 slaves, who toiled in the silver mines at Lavrion, to a Thracian entrepreneur at one obol per day per head (Xenophon *Poroi* 4.14). His name was also found on *ostraka*, which was the ultimate cachet for any Athenian politician worth his salt.

However, Nikias was in nearly every way the opposite of Alcibiades. Older than his rival by 20 years, Nikias was particularly cautious and notoriously superstitious. Whereas Alcibiades liked to dazzle the Athenian people, Nikias was careful to ascribe his success to the favour of the gods in order to avoid provoking envy. More importantly, Alcibiades saw the by now protracted war against the Spartans as a splendid opportunity for the aggrandizement of himself and of his city; Nikias, it seems, longed only to end it. In 421 BC he succeeded temporarily in doing so.

Nikias had been a highly successful *stratêgos* in the first decade of the Peloponnesian War, most notably capturing the islands of Minoa, which lay just off Megara, and Kythera, off the southern coast of Lakonia (3.51,

4.53–54). In the winter of 422/421 BC he was prominent in the negotiations for peace between Athens and Sparta, and Thucydides analyzes his motives for being so:

> So now, while still untouched by misfortune and still held in honour, Nikias wished to rest upon his laurels, to find an immediate release from toil and trouble both for himself and for his fellow citizens, and to leave behind him the name of one whose service to the state had been successful from start to finish. He thought that these ends were to be achieved by avoiding all risks and by trusting oneself as little as possible to fortune, and that risks could be avoided only in peace. (5.16.1)

This man, rich, conscientious, and interested chiefly in preserving his good reputation, was ultimately to die with his troops in Sicily.

Yet most Athenians regarded his superstitious nature as a joke. Aristophanes poked fun of it in his comedy *Amphiaraos*, produced at the time, in the summer of 414 BC, when hopes were still running high for the success of the Sicilian expedition. Similarly in *The Birds*, staged earlier in the same year, Aristophanes had even gone so far as to coin the verb 'delay like Nikias' (*mellonikiao*: line 640). But, as will be related, when these characteristics combined to work in tandem and influence Nikias' military judgement, disaster would follow for the Athenians sitting outside Syracuse.

Lamachos (d. 414 BC)
Lamachos son of Xenophanes, an experienced soldier, was about 50 years of age when he was elected as the third of the three *stratêgoi* for the Sicilian expedition. Oddly enough, Aristophanes had presented him as something of a young braggart soldier in *The Acharnians*, produced early in 425 BC, and teased him about his poverty (lines 568–625).

Lamachos was a *stratêgos* in 435 BC or thereabouts, led a detachment of ten ships into the Black Sea in 424 BC, the same year Thucydides was assigned to command a similar detachment near Amphipolis in Thrace, and was one of the signatories to the Peace of Nikias in 421 BC (4.75.1, 5.19.2). Lamachos, as we shall see, was not averse to taking soldierly risks.

Daring to the end, Lamachos probably died the way he would have wished, leading his men in a charge. According to Thucydides (6.101.6) he was killed when he and a handful of his men found themselves isolated and surrounded by enemy horsemen. Plutarch, on the other hand, elaborates upon this version by saying a Syracusan cavalry officer, Kallikrates, challenged him to a duel and he accepted. Seemingly Lamachos 'came forward and received the first thrust, but he succeeded in closing with his adversary and returning the blow, so that he and Kallikrates fell together'(Plutarch *Nikias* 18.2). True or not, it is fitting that Aristophanes makes a nostalgic reference to 'hero Lamachos' in *Frogs* (line 1039) produced in 405 BC.

Demosthenes (d. 413 BC)
Demosthenes, son of Alkisthenes, was an energetic *stratêgos* with experience of both land and sea operations. After a disastrously impetuous foray into Aetolia in 426 BC (3.94–98), Demosthenes had redeemed himself by saving the Athenian naval base at Naupaktos, and then by defeating the Peloponnesian forces when they invaded Akarnania. In 425 BC Demosthenes had been the prime mover behind the defeat of the Spartans at Pylos, and he

had fought at Megara and in Thrace the following year. Although, like Lamachos, he was one of the signatories to the Peace of Nikias in 421 BC (5.19.2), he had participated in Alcibiades' Peloponnesian venture in 418 BC. Since he was tough, energetic and battle-hardened, there would have been justifiable hope that he would be able to restore the situation outside Syracuse when he was elected *stratêgos*, along with Eurymedon, to lead the second expedition to Sicily.

Eurymedon (d. 413 BC)

Eurymedon son of Thoukles first looms large as a *stratêgos* commanding a fleet of 60 triremes during the Corcyraean civil war of 427 BC. His arrival encouraged the democrats to finish off their oligarchic opponents, for during the seven days the Athenian fleet was there 'the Corcyraeans continued to massacre those of their own citizens whom they considered their enemies' (3.81.4). The following year he was one of *stratêgoi* elected to command the intervention force in Sicily. When, however, the Siciliote Greeks themselves decided to settle their differences in the summer of 424 BC an Athenian presence became both unnecessary and undesirable; when the Athenians did withdraw, Eurymedon was indicted on the spurious charge of having been bribed to leave Sicily (4.65.3). It was Nikias who brought these trumped-up charges against him and, ironically as it would turn out, it would be Nikias who would be hoist by his own petard outside Syracuse.

Alcibiades

A ward of Perikles and student of Sokrates, the flamboyant Alcibiades ranked amongst the most popular, handsome young aristocrats of democratic Athens. The golden boy of Athens' golden age, posterity would remember him as the most notorious double turncoat in Greek history. Known for winning chariot races at Olympia, Alcibiades persuaded the assembly to let him assume control of the Peloponnesian War after his rival Nikias opted for peace with Sparta. 'It is agreed by all who have written his biography', wrote Cornelius Nepos, 'that he was never excelled either in faults or in virtues' (*Alcibiades* 1.1).

On the eve of the departure of the fleet for Sicily, all the Herms (square pillars of stone bearing the head and erect phallus of the god Hermes, protector of voyagers among other things) across Athens were defaced and castrated (6.27.1–2) and Alcibiades was implicated. As reputed ringleader of the Herm-Choppers (*Hermokopidai*), whose impious vandalism had thrown the city into such a state of frenzy, the assembly issued orders recalling Alcibiades to Athens. His enemies brought forward fresh indictments, including profanation of the Eleusian Mysteries, when Alcibiades and others of his circle had donned mock-sacral garments and had amused themselves by presiding over sham initiations in irreverence of the grain-goddess Demeter and her daughter Persephone.

These offences were cited not merely as outrages against the gods, meriting death on that account alone, but as evidence of their perpetrators' contempt for democracy itself. They were the acts of a revolutionary, a would-be tyrant who set himself above all law. He managed to jump ship and vanish. And so just three months after he had sailed from Athens with such pomp and splendour he was a renegade, a hunted man with a price on his head. When the fugitive heard his fellow citizens had condemned him to death, he apparently remarked, 'I'll show them that I am still alive' (Plutarch *Alcibiades* 22.2).

The fortification walls at Temenites, the sacred area dedicated to Apollo, looking west from the theatre. The smaller wall to the front of the larger one is probably the 'winter wall' hurriedly built by the Syracusans over the winter of 415/414 BC. (Fields-Carré Collection)

He next washed up in Sparta, where he convinced the ordinarily canny Spartans to intervene in Sicily and preserve their fellow Dorians of Syracuse. Gylippos' mission, as we shall see, was the result. He also persuaded them to change their strategy for winning the war with Athens. Instead of annual invasions of its home territory by land during the campaigning season, the Spartans now fortified Dekeleia in north-eastern Attica, which they garrisoned year round. The site chosen commanded a view southwards over the plain of Attica as far as the Peiraieus, and the garrison put tremendous pressure on the Athenians. It cut their land route through Oropos to the island of Euboia, where they had sent much of their sheep and cattle. The fort also provided a place of refuge for runaway slaves working in the silver mines at Lavrion on the southern tip of Attica, 20,000 of whom took the opportunity to hotfoot it to Dekeleia.

THE SYRACUSANS

Syracuse had experienced a period of rule by tyrants under whom the *polis* established a political supremacy over the rest of Sicily. Then, in 467 BC, it went democratic, and by the 440s began to coerce its neighbours in an organized way. Indeed, Syracuse had a democracy and foreign policy similar to that of Athens, and one of the leading themes of Thucydides' account of the Sicilian expedition is the similarity between the two antagonists.

Hermokrates (d. 408 BC)
At the debate in Kamarina, when Syracuse and Athens were competing for the support of Kamarina when the issue of the expedition was still in the balance, Hermokrates son of Hermon made a full-frontal assault on Athenian imperialism. He did so by castigating Athens for fighting on behalf of Leontinoi, 'and meanwhile to be holding down in subjection the actual inhabitants of Chalkis in Euboia, whose colonists the Leontinians are' (6.76.1). The seemingly broad-minded delegate from Syracuse then savagely condemned Athens' argument that it protected Greek states from Persian aggression, which was nothing but a cloak as Athens wanted to substitute its

empire for that of Persia. Athenian imperialism, according to Hermokrates, meant the enslavement of allies.

Thucydides openly admires Hermokrates' intellectual and moral qualities and capacity for leadership (6.72.3), and had already brought him to prominence as the man chiefly responsible for persuading the Siciliote Greeks to close ranks against the Athenians in 424 BC (4.58–65). He had addressed the gathering at the Gela congress claiming to speak not in the interest of his own city but for all Sicily, accusing Athens of evil designs against the whole island. Sincere or not, it would be Hermokrates who was the prime mover behind the resistance to the Athenian armada.

In the summer of 412 BC Hermokrates was sent as commander of a fleet of 22 triremes to co-operate with the Spartans in the eastern Aegean (8.26.1), and while there learned he had been deposed and banished by the popular vote (Thucydides 8.85.3, Xenophon *Hellenika* 1.1.27). It seems Syracuse was now run by a more radically democratic regime, which had come to power after a revolution connected with the Athenian defeat (Aristotle *Politics* 1304a 27). Ironically, the outcome of the fight to the death between Syracuse and Athens was a destabilization of democratic politics at both places: victory led Syracuse to switch to a more extreme democracy, defeat led Athens to a temporary switch to oligarchy.

The exiled Hermokrates, who returned to the eastern Aegean in a private capacity (Xenophon *Hellenika* 1.3.13), was to eventually lose his life in street fighting at Syracuse. In 408/407 BC Hermokrates attempted a *coup d'état*, but failed. One of his henchmen was a young man by the name of Dionysios. He survived, albeit badly wounded, and two years later he himself seized power as tyrant, taking advantage of the recent Carthaginian success at Akragas and the subsequent political chaos in Syracuse (Diodoros 13.91.3–4). The democratic interlude was not merely short but atypical; in Syracuse, one-man rule was the norm.

Gylippos (fl. 414–404 BC)

As a product of Sparta, not Syracuse, Gylippos was the closest to what we would consider a professional soldier, and would turn what seemed like an inevitable Syracusan defeat into a resounding victory. Gylippos, whose birth date is not recorded, was brought up in penury. He was the son of the Kleandridas who in 446 BC was adviser to King Pleistoanax of Sparta, on the occasion of his sudden unexplained withdrawal from Attica (Plutarch *Perikles* 22.3, cf. Thucydides 1.114.2, 2.21.1). Accused of having taken bribes from the agents of Perikles, Kleandridas fled to Thourioi (Sibari), a pan-Hellenic colony then being founded in the instep of Italy with Athenian help and participation. What is more, Gylippos' mother, it was said, was a helot, which meant he was not a true Spartiate but a *mothax*, a man of inferior status. Despite this, however, from an early childhood he was trained for war in the traditional Spartan fashion and on reaching maturity had been elected to a military mess, his dues contributed by a wealthier Spartiate patron. For an individual of marginal origins, war was an opportunity to gain honour and eminence.

It is significant that Gylippos became famous as a result of being sent to Sicily, where he never commanded full Spartan citizens, or Spartiates. He was possibly chosen as an ad hoc generalissimo because of his family connections with Thourioi. Condemned to death in his absence, Kleandridas nevertheless survived to help the men of Thourioi in a war against the Tarentines. Curiously, however, after his outstanding performance at Syracuse Gylippos hardly features again in our historical record. That said, it was alleged that he stole money from Lysandros, which the admiral had entrusted to him. Like father like son, it seems, 'for Gylippos himself, after his brilliant exploits, was also convicted of taking bribes and banished from Sparta in disgrace' (Plutarch *Perikles* 22.4, cf. *Lysandros* 16). An alternative version of the story has Gylippos starving himself to death 'after he had been found guilty by the ephors of filching from the money of Lysandros' (Athenaios 6.24). Exile or starvation, either way it was a sad demise for the audacious Gylippos.

OPPOSING ARMIES

The *polis* (pl. *poleis*), or the 'city-state', was the characteristic form of Greek urban life. Its main features were small size, political autonomy, social homogeneity, and a real sense of community and respect for law. Yet the *polis* was not really a city, nor was it simply a town as its population was distributed over a rural territory that might include many villages. It also emphasized people, the citizens, rather than territory. The distinctive sense of the *polis* was, therefore, a 'citizen-state' rather than a 'city-state'.

As the *polis* was always defined in terms of its members (e.g. the Athenians not Athens, the Syracusans not Syracuse), rather than geographically, it was, in essence, a community of warrior-farmers, males of military age who would necessarily fight for it, in which the military power of the community controlled the political and institutional life (magistracies, council, assembly). Because it was an agrarian-based society, the *polis* itself controlled and exploited a territory (*chôra*), which was farmed by the citizens and their households. As the *chôra* was delimited geographically by mountains or sea, or by proximity to another *polis*, parochial border wars were common. Autonomy was jealously guarded, but the necessities of collaboration made for a proliferation of foreign alliances, leagues, and hegemonies.

CITIZEN-MILITIA

The armies of Greek *poleis* were based on a levy of those citizens (*politês*) prosperous enough to equip themselves as hoplites, heavily armoured infantry who fought shoulder to shoulder in a large formation known as a phalanx – the word means 'stacks' or 'rows' of men. Except for the Spartans, who devoted their entire lives to military training, and a few state-sponsored units such as the famous homoerotic unit, the Theban Sacred Band of 300 men who were bound together by homosexual pairing, these citizen levies were untrained part-time soldiers. As a citizen of a *polis* it was your moral, social and, above all, political duty to fight on behalf of your state in times of war. Liable for military service at any time from the age of 20, citizens remained on the state muster rolls for at least 40 years – desertion or cowardice could lead to loss of citizenship – and even a tragic poet such as the Athenian Aischylos stood in the phalanx, and was, in fact, to be remembered on his grave as a warrior, not as the first great tragedian.

The Athenians, famously, went the whole hog, and made the people sovereign. All Athenian citizens, that is, freeborn native males of military age, had the right, and indeed obligation, to attend the assembly and vote on its

proposals, just as they had the right and obligation to bear arms. To most people nowadays classical Athens may seem the least alien of all ancient states and in some respects the Athenians went beyond even modern democracies in achieving Lincoln's ideal of 'government of the people, by the people, for the people'. But Athens was also a slave-owning state, and, for much of the classical period, an imperialist state; many contemporary analysts regarded democracy as a bad thing, if not an absurdity.

ABOVE, LEFT
A Corinthian helmet (London, British Museum, GR 1814.7-4.973) of the very elegant 'final form' (*c.* 460 BC). Beaten out of a single sheet of bronze, it was shaped to the skull with only small openings for the eyes, nostrils and mouth. (Fields-Carré Collection)

ABOVE, CENTRE
A 5th-century Attic helmet (London, British Museum, GR 1883.12-8.3). This helmet type featured large cut-outs for the eyes and ears, and rounded, hinged cheek pieces. It was similar to the Chalcidian helmet, but without the short nose guard. (Fields-Carré Collection)

ABOVE, RIGHT
A pair of bronze greaves (London, British Museum, GR 1856.12-26.710) patently once gilded (*c.* 520 BC). Though cumbersome to wear, greaves protected the shins and followed the musculature of the calf. They were kept in place by the natural springiness of the bronze. (Fields-Carré Collection)

PANOPLY

Although it seems that hoplites were experimenting with lighter equipment by the time of the Peloponnesian War, the basic hoplite panoply (*panopliâ*) remained a large, round soup-bowl shaped shield (*aspis*), approximately a metre in diameter, a bronze helmet, some form of body armour, and bronze greaves. The whole, if worn, could weigh in excess of 30kg, the heaviest individual item being the *aspis* at 7kg or thereabouts.

Built on a wooden core, the *aspis* was faced with an extremely thin layer of stressed bronze and backed by a leather lining. The core was usually crafted from flexible wood such as poplar or willow. Because of its great weight the shield was carried by an arrangement of two handles, the armband (*porpax*) in the centre through which the forearm passed and the handgrip (*antilabê*) at the rim. Held across the chest, it covered the hoplite from chin to knee. However, being clamped to the left arm it only offered protection to the hoplite's left-hand side.

Above the flat, broad rim of the shield, the hoplite's head was fully protected by a helmet, hammered from a single sheet of bronze, the favoured Corinthian style. It had a long life – the true Corinthian helmet continues down to about 400 BC – as it covered the face leaving only small openings for the eyes, nostrils and mouth, and yielded to a blow without cracking. A leather lining was fixed to the interior by the small holes pierced in the metal. Under the helmet many men wore a headband, which not only restrained the hair but also provided some support for this heavy piece of armour. Nevertheless, any hoplite wearing a padded bronze helmet in a hot climate was quite prepared to suffer considerable discomfort. Out of battle the helmet could be pushed to the back of the head, leaving the face uncovered. Other helmet types, which provided good vision but left the face exposed in battle, included the Chalcidian and Attic types.

Although it has been suggested that the only armour carried in this period was the *aspis*, Thucydides repeatedly indicates that hoplites still wore some kind of body armour, perhaps of leather or linen, and a pair of bronze greaves

(*knemides*) to protect the lower legs. First appearing in around 525 BC, the great advantage of the linen corselet (*linothôrax*) was its comfort, as it was more flexible and much cooler than bronze under the Mediterranean sun. It was made up of many layers of linen glued together with resin to form a stiff shirt, about half a centimetre thick. Below the waist it was cut into strips (*pteruges*) for ease of movement, with a second layer of *pteruges* being fixed behind the first, thereby covering the gaps between them and forming a kind of kilt that protected the groin. A linen corselet would not deflect glancing blows, but it would be as effective as bronze against any major thrust.

The weapon par excellence of the hoplite was the long-thrusting spear (*doru*). Fashioned out of ash wood and some 2 to 2.5m in length, the *doru* was equipped with a bronze or iron spearhead and bronze butt-spike. As well as acting as a counterweight to the spearhead, the butt-spike, affectionately known as the 'lizard-killer' (*sauroter*), allowed the spear to be planted in the ground when a hoplite was ordered to ground arms (being bronze it did not rust), or to fight with if his spear snapped in the mêlée. The weapon was usually thrust overarm, the spear tip to the face of the foe, although it could be easily thrust underarm if the hoplite was charging into contact at the run. The centre of the shaft was bound in cord for a secure grip. The hoplite also carried a sword (*kopis*), usually a heavy, one-edged blade designed for slashing with an overhand stroke. Both the cutting edge and the back were convex, weighing the weapon towards the tip, but this was very much a secondary weapon.

TACTICS

It was the hoplite shield that made the rigid phalanx formation viable. Half the shield protruded beyond the left-hand side of the hoplite. If the man on the left moved in close he was protected by the shield overlap, which thus guarded his uncovered side. Hence, hoplites stood shoulder to shoulder with their shields locked. Once this formation was broken, however, the advantage of the shield was lost; as Plutarch says (*Moralia* 241) the body armour of a hoplite may be for the individual's protection, but the hoplite's shield protected the whole phalanx.

The phalanx itself was a deep formation, normally composed of hoplites stacked eight to twelve shields deep. In this dense mass only the front two ranks could use their spears in the mêlée, the men in ranks three and back adding weight to the attack by pushing to their front. This was probably achieved by shoving the man in front with your shield. Both Thucydides (4.43.3, 96.4) and Xenophon (*Hellenika* 4.3.19, 6.4.14) commonly refer to the push and shove (*ôthismos*) of a hoplite mêlée.

In hoplite warfare, therefore, the phalanx was the tactic. When one *polis* engaged another, the crucial battle would usually be fought on flatland with mutually visible fronts that were not more than a kilometre or so long and often only a few hundred metres apart. Normally, after a final blood sacrifice

The double-gripped, concave *aspis*, seen here on the Nereid monument (London, British Museum, 859), was singular. Phalanxes were calibrated by the depth of their cumulative shields – 'eight-shields deep', 'twelve-shields deep' – not by counting spears. Note the shield-to-shield position. (Fields-Carré Collection)

(*sphagia*), the two opposing phalanxes would simply head straight for each other, break into a trot for the last few metres, collide with a crash and then, blinded by the dust and their own cumbersome helmets, stab and shove until one side cracked.

Thucydides properly devotes a sizeable portion of his work to the encounter at Mantineia where, in the summer of 418 BC, Athens with its democratic allies of Argos and the rebel Peloponnesian *polis* of Mantineia took on the might of Sparta and its Peloponnesian League. Indeed, this is one of the best descriptions we have of a hoplite battle. One of the telling explanatory details he provides for his readers (5.71.1) is the fact that the hoplite phalanx, as it advanced into contact, tended to edge to the right. The right-hand man would drift in fear of being caught on his unshielded side, and the rest of the phalanx would naturally follow suit, each hoplite trying to keep under the protection of his right-hand neighbour's shield. Thus each right wing might overlap and beat the opposing left. Thucydides implies that this was a tendency over which *stratêgoi* had little or no control.

A 5th-century Attic grave stele (Athens, National Archaeological Museum, 3379). The *aspis* covered the bearer from chin to knee, and more than anything else made the phalanx possible. Note the flat, offset rim, which provided rigidity to the bowl. (Fields-Carré Collection)

Hand-to-hand combat, close-quarter fighting, coming to grips or to blows, the Greeks delicately called all this the 'law of hands' (Herodotos 8.89.1). The mêlée itself was a toe-to-toe affair, the front two ranks of opposing phalanxes attempting to stab their spears into the exposed parts of the enemy, that is, the throat or groin, which lacked protection. Meanwhile, the ranks behind would push. As can be imagined, once a hoplite was down, injured or not, he was unlikely ever to get up again. This short but vicious mêlée was resolved once one side had practically collapsed. There was no pursuit by the victors, and those of the vanquished who were able fled the battlefield. It was enough, as the philosophers noted, every so often to kill a small portion of the enemy in an afternoon crash, crack his morale, and send him scurrying in defeat and shame whence he came. The basic concept in hoplite warfare was the domination of the battlefield and not the extermination of the enemy.

Othismos

The opposing phalanxes would collide head to head, the front rank of each usually falling at the onset. Xenophon, in his eye-witness account of the battle of Second Koroneia (394 BC), laconically recalls:

> [Agesilaos' phalanx] crashed into the Thebans front to front. So with shield pressed against shield (*ôthismos aspidon*) they struggled, killed and were killed. (Xenophon *Hellenika* 4.3.19)

At the battle of Delion (424 BC), according to Thucydides, the Thebans 'got the better of the Athenians, pushing them back (*ôthismos aspidon*) step by step at first and keeping up their pressure' (4.96.4). Once experienced, such a thing was never easily forgotten and even Aristophanes' chorus of veteran hoplites is made to say:

A phalanx, in a scene from the Nereid monument (London, British Museum, 868). In the front rank, fifth from the left, is a hoplite with his head turned to the right. He may be a *stratêgos* encouraging his men as they advance into contact. (Fields-Carré Collection)

[A]fter running out with the spear and shield, we fought them… each man stood up against each man… we pushed them with the gods until evening. (Aristophanes *Wasps* 1081–85)

The pushing with the shields explains the famous cry of the Theban *stratêgos*, Epameinondas, 'for one more pace' (Polyainos 2.3.2) at Leuktra (371 BC). Indeed, Xenophon, who was no admirer of the Thebans, says that the Spartan right at Leuktra was 'pushed back' (*Hellenika* 6.4.14). Xenophon advocates that the best men should be placed in front and at the rear of a phalanx so that the worse men in the middle, namely the cowards and the like, could be 'led by the former and pushed by the latter' (*Memorabilia* 3.1.18).

The pushing itself could go on for some time. Thucydides says that at the battle of Solygeia (425 BC) the Athenian and Karystian right wing 'with difficulty pushed the Corinthians back' (4.43.3). However, once one side collapsed, all was up; long-range pursuit was not in the lexicon of hoplite warfare.

RITUAL

Hoplite battles had a strong ritual character; the idea was to defeat rather than to annihilate. Hoplites fought a set-piece battle on the flattest piece of terrain and physically pushed the enemy from the pitch, a point clearly made by the Persian commander, Mardonios, in a speech to his cousin, King Xerxes:

[T]he Greeks are pugnacious enough, and start fights on the spur of the moment without sense or judgement to justify them. When they declare war on each other, they go off together to the smoothest and flattest piece of ground they can find, and have their battle on it. (Herodotos 7.9B.1)

Although Mardonios believed that the Greeks pursued their unique style of warfare out of ignorance and stupidity, what he says is incontrovertible. As it turned out, he would lose both his life and his army on a distant plain in Boiotia.

But why did the hoplite style of head-to-head, open-terrain fighting last so long? For a start, the fighting was taking place on the hoplites' own land. However, as time passed the system was maintained for the sake of tradition, shared values and social prejudice. Hoplite warfare was for prestige rather than for the survival of a *polis*. Sparta, whose warriors were acknowledged as the past masters of this style of warfare, was an exception to the rule: its hoplites were permanent and essential rather than occasional and ritual. The Spartans, ever conservative, also retained their two hereditary kings, but only as commanders-in-chief.

Indeed, there were implicit rules of engagement, the 'common customs', for Greeks fighting Greeks. These rules include the following: war was to be declared before hostilities; hostilities were sometimes inappropriate (e.g. during religious festivals); some places were protected, and some persons (e.g. shrines, heralds); trophies were respected; the dead were to be returned; non-combatants were not a legitimate target; fighting was to take place in the proper season; and there was to be a limited pursuit of defeated and retreating foes. These rules did not apply to 'barbarians', non-Greek speakers, and they would break down during the Peloponnesian War, a war unprecedented in scale, duration, and barbarity.

Euripides' tragedy the *Suppliants*, produced at Athens within a year of its shattering defeat at Delion, was prompted by the barbaric Theban treatment of the Athenians left for dead on the battlefield. The length and ferocity of this 'world-wide' struggle would transform warfare from a seasonal activity to one in which at least low-level conflict lasted throughout the traditionally inactive winter months. Low-level conflict was in fact characteristic of most of the war, on the Athenian side, for instance, taking the form of seaborne raids on the Peloponnese. Only two large hoplite battles were fought, Delion and Mantineia. As we shall discover, there were also large-scale engagements by the Athenians encamped outside Syracuse, but for the most part the traditional decisive encounter did not take place. In actual fact, the final destruction of the Athenian invaders would be brought about by hoplites operating in close conjunction with lightly armed troops and cavalry.

CAVALRY

In ancient Greece suitable land for horses was confined to an area stretching northwards from Boiotia. Athens' own territory and much of Greece to the south of Attica was unsuitable. In particular, the limited water and fodder supply in most of Greece during the campaigning season limited the

Information about the Athenian cavalry corps is fuller than that for any other *polis*. A fraction of the army, its young aristocratic members are peculiarly conspicuous in the Parthenon frieze (London, British Museum, north XXXVIII), the so-called flagship monument of democracy. (Fields-Carré Collection)

usefulness of cavalry. The contrast with the Greek colonies of the west, which had such resources, is clear from the archaeological record. The majority of finds of an equestrian nature occur in southern Italy and Sicily. In general, most of the mainland *poleis* did not have the resources to devote to supporting horse-rearing on a large scale.

Greek cavalry suffered from technical limitations that further reduced its advantages compared to hoplite forces. Greek horses in the classical period were small by both medieval and modern standards, and were limited in the weight they could carry. This obviously restricted the amount of armour carried by both horse and rider. In addition, the Greeks lacked horseshoes, a liability in a land as rough as Greece. It is noticeable that Xenophon, an expert in equestrian matters, is very concerned with the feet of cavalry mounts and the possibilities that horses would be lame. These limitations tended to hamper the operational range of horses, to turn cavalry away from the use of shock weapons, and to promote the employment of missile weapons such as the javelin.

Such troops could not ride down hoplites, provided at least they kept their formation. But they were useful for flank or rear attacks and for protecting their own formations from similar enemy action. They were also effective against hoplites once their phalanx had been broken or in harassing them on the march and in cutting off stragglers. Cavalry could threaten the enemy's food supply by preventing foraging. Greek cavalry could hold its own against lightly armed troops if properly handled. Further, its usefulness for reconnaissance, patrolling, picket duty and forming a cavalry screen for the main formations was recognized and utilized in this period.

Horsemen of Athens

The Athenians only instituted a proper cavalry corps after the Persian Wars, its members being recruited from those wealthy enough to maintain a horse. And so, by the mid-5th century BC there was a body of 300 (Andokides 3.5), rising either to 1,200 (Thucydides 2.13.8) or 1,000 (Aristophanes *Knights* 225) by the start of the Peloponnesian War. This makes the tiny number (30) of the initial cavalry force sent by the Athenians as part of the expeditionary force to Sicily something of a mystery.

Owning a horse was very costly; Aristotle remarks that 'horse-breeding requires the ownership of large resources' (*Politics* 1321a 11). Xenophon also stresses the need for 'ample means' (*Peri Hippikes* 2.1), and adds that such men should also have an interest in the affairs of the state. The members of the cavalry corps, therefore, were drawn mainly from the second of Solon's four property classes, the *hippeis*, comprising citizens whose land yielded between 300 and 500 measures (*medimnoi*) of grain or the equivalent in other produce (Anon, *Athenaiôn politeia* 7.3-4). According to Xenophon (*Hipparchikos* 1.11) preparation for service in the cavalry corps began

A fragmentary relief (Athens, Agora Museum, I 7167) commemorating a tribal victory in the *anthippasia*, a mock cavalry battle (*c.* 400 BC). The Athenian cavalry corps was made up of ten units, one from each tribe. The bearded rider is obviously an officer. (Fields-Carré Collection)

while a youth was still under the control of his legal guardian, in other words before the age of 18.

Citizens were organized into ten tribes at Athens, and each of these furnished a tribe (*phyle*) of horsemen commanded by a *phylarchos* (Xenophon *Hipparchikos* 2.2). The ten *phylai* of horse were under the overall command of two *hipparchoi*, each of whom would command in battle a wing made up of five *phylai* (Anon. *Athenaiôn politeia* 61.4). Like the *stratêgoi*, all these officers would be annually elected by the assembly, the two *hipparchoi* from the whole citizen body and the *phylarchoi* one from each tribe (Anon. *Athenaiôn politeia* 1.3, 61.4-5). As service in the military was a normal duty of citizenship, the horsemen, like the hoplites, were not paid a regular wage, but unlike the hoplites they were given an allowance of one *drachma* per day for fodder in times of war. On entering service with the cavalry corps the young aristocrat would also be paid an establishment grant (*katastasis*) to cover the cost of his mount, which, along with his equipment, he provided himself. The grant had to be paid back on leaving the corps, unless the mount had been killed or crippled during active service.

To avoid fraudulent claiming of allowances an inspection (*dokimasia*) was performed annually by the *boulê*, following the election of the officers. Each rider and horse would be scrutinized for fitness for service. Mounts that failed to pass the inspection were branded on the jaw with the sign of a wheel in order to prevent them being slipped through on another occasion (Anon. *Athenaiôn politeia* 49.1). If passed, the riders' names would be entered on the cavalry list, which would be passed on to the ten *taxiarchoi*, the commanders of the ten tribal *taxeis* into which the citizen-hoplites were divided, and like the *stratêgoi*, elected by the assembly. The *taxiarchoi* would delete the names of those entered on the cavalry list from the tribal recruitment rolls to ensure that no one became liable for both hoplite and mounted service.

Attic red-figure pelike (Athens, National Archaeological Museum, 1333) dated to *c.* 400 BC. This youthful horsemen, capped with a *petasos* or Thessalian sun hat, is wielding a *doratus kamakinou* – a long, thin spear appropriate for 'pig-sticking' enemy infantry. (Fields-Carré Collection)

Horsemen of Syracuse

During the Sicilian expedition the Campanian Greeks dispatched cavalry to help the Athenians (Diodoros 13.44.1–2, not in Thucydides) and, broadly speaking, the cavalry forces of the western Greek *poleis* were more developed and effective than those of mainland Greece. In the words of the early 5th-century Theban poet, Pindar:

> The son of Kronos [Zeus] has honoured Sicily, rich with the wealthy summits of its cities. In addition he has given a people of horsemen, suitors of bronze-armoured war. (Pindar *Nemean* 1.15–19)

The superiority of Syracusan cavalry was to play a vital role in the total defeat of the Athenian expeditionary force.

Comprehensive information on the Syracusan army as such is somewhat scrappy. Thucydides' account of the expedition, unsurprisingly, is presented

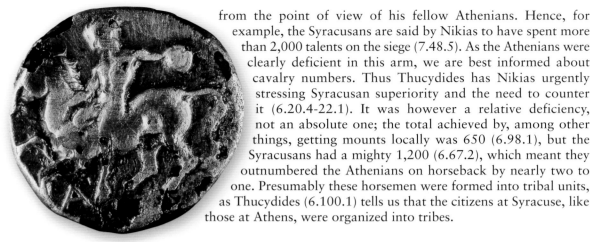

from the point of view of his fellow Athenians. Hence, for example, the Syracusans are said by Nikias to have spent more than 2,000 talents on the siege (7.48.5). As the Athenians were clearly deficient in this arm, we are best informed about cavalry numbers. Thus Thucydides has Nikias urgently stressing Syracusan superiority and the need to counter it (6.20.4-22.1). It was however a relative deficiency, not an absolute one; the total achieved by, among other things, getting mounts locally was 650 (6.98.1), but the Syracusans had a mighty 1,200 (6.67.2), which meant they outnumbered the Athenians on horseback by nearly two to one. Presumably these horsemen were formed into tribal units, as Thucydides (6.100.1) tells us that the citizens at Syracuse, like those at Athens, were organized into tribes.

A Tarentine silver *didrachma* (Vlasto 1947: 435), dated to *c.* 380–345 BC. Western Greek cavalry were more developed and effective than those of mainland Greece, and it is noteworthy that the horsemen of Taras were the first to use the shield on horseback. (Franco Taccogna)

LIGHTLY ARMED TROOPS

Citizen-hoplites were not only supported by the mounted arm drawn from the wealthier citizens of a *polis*, but also by the poorer property classes that would serve as lightly armed troops. Additionally, lightly armed troops could be recruited as allies or mercenaries from the more mountainous areas of central Greece, such as Aetolia, Akarnania, and from the relatively backward states around the Thessalian plain, or from areas peripheral to the main centres of power, like Crete or Rhodes. Non-Greeks were also utilized, the best attested being the Thracians.

On pottery, Attic red-figure particularly, lightly armed troops are normally shown wearing the everyday dress of Greek shepherds, namely a tunic of coarse cloth and a shaggy felt hat. Wearing no armour, their sole means of defence was a makeshift shield formed by an animal pelt laid across the left arm and secured into place by knotting a pair of the paws around the neck. Lacking the specialist training to use bow or sling, weapons seem to be restricted to stones or javelins; only occasionally do we find the odd representation of a figure carrying a sword.

A javelin was provided with a leather thong (*ankyle*) midway along the shaft. The thong would be fixed on to the shaft with a temporary hitch knot and formed a loop that was hooked round the index finger of the thrower; it fell off the javelin when it was launched and was, consequently, retained in the hand. The throwing-thong imparted extra speed to the javelin as well as rotation for stability in flight. Thucydides (3.97.3-98.2) gives us a vivid picture of the Aetolian javelineers, whom the Athenians suspected of eating raw meat, picking off 'by far the best men in the city of Athens that fell during this war' (3.98.4) when Demosthenes led a force of hoplites into the Aetolian mountains during the summer of 426 BC.

Slingers were also commonly used in Greek armies, being either drawn from the poorer citizens of the *polis*, or being hired as mercenaries. The most renowned slingers came from Rhodes, and Thucydides (6.43.2) says the Athenians hired 700 of them specifically for their craft for the Sicilian expedition. Thucydides (2.81.8) also mentions the Akarnanians as expert slingers. Like other Greek lightly armed troops, slingers wore no armour. They could serve as a complement to archers, and their weapons could not only out-range the bow but they could also carry a larger supply of ammunition than archers.

The sling bullets were invariably small stones or pebbles, though those of the Rhodians were of lead, almond shaped, and weighing some 20–30g. These leaden bullets, the most effective of slingshots, were often cast bearing messages to the recipient, such as 'take that', while other extant examples include '[this one's] for you', 'ouch', and 'get pregnant with this'. Xenophon says (*Anabasis* 3.3.16) that these easily out-ranged the large stones shot from Persian slings, and were even able to out-range most enemy archers. This suggests the maximum range of Rhodian slingshot was possibly as much as 350m.

The bow was not a usual Greek weapon – in Homer's *Iliad* it is only used by one or two heroes on either side – and there is some suggestion that archers were generally despised. However, during the Persian Wars the Athenians deployed a small unit of citizen-archers (Herodotos 9.22, 60), and by the Peloponnesian War both mounted and foot-archers (2.13.8). Athens also maintained at state expense a small force of Scythian archers, but these northern 'barbarians' were mainly used for police duties within the city proper or for service with the fleet. They wore a distinctive long pointed hat and colourful loose-fitting trousers that are widely reproduced in contemporary Attic vase-paintings.

An Attic red-figure *pelike* (Siracusa, Museo Archeologico Regionale, 9317) dated to 430 BC. Supporting the 'heroically nude' hoplite is a lightly armed soldier. He wears a *pilos* helmet and wields a javelin but, unlike the hoplite, he lacks a secondary weapon. (Fields-Carré Collection)

The Greeks themselves used a self-bow made of a single flexible wooden staff. Cretan archers, on the other hand, who were specialists and thus often hired as mercenaries, used the composite bow, as did Scythian archers. Like other areas that supplied mercenaries, Crete suffered from political instability as well as from excess population and endemic warfare. If Pausanias (4.8.3), writing in the mid-2nd century AD, is trustworthy, Cretan specialization in archery goes back to the 8th century BC, a time when the use of the bow on the mainland was declining.

The composite bow itself consisted of a wooden core onto which was laminated sinew (front) and horn (back). The elasticity of the sinew meant that when the bow was drawn it stretched and was put under tension. By contrast, the strips of horn were compressed. By exploiting their mechanical properties, both materials thus reacted to propel the bowstring. This type of bow was very difficult to string and required the use both of legs and arms.

Scythian arrows were short with small tips, unlike the heavy arrowheads of the Cretans, but in his capacious bow case (*gorytos*) he carried both his bow and a great many diminutive arrows. Herodotos says (4.64) human skin, from enemy limbs, was favoured for covering the bow case because of its whiteness. When firing, the Scythians employed the Mediterranean loose that is used by western archers today. In this they contrasted with the normal Greek practice, which was to pinch the arrow between thumb and forefinger, a weak grip that meant that Greeks, apart from our Cretan specialists, were unable to draw the powerful composite bows of the Scythians. This may in part explain why the full value of archers was only gradually appreciated in Greece towards the end of the Peloponnesian War.

Of all the lightly armed troops used in Greek armies the peltast (*peltastês*) was the most effective. He was named after the small wicker shield (*peltê*) he carried. According to Aristotle it was rimless and covered with 'goatskin or the like' (fr. 498 Rose). Although he implies that the shield was round, in art it is depicted as crescent shaped, a segment being cut out of the top edge. The peltast was of Thracian origin and, as described by both Herodotos (7.75) and Xenophon (*Anabasis* 7.4.4), wore the traditional costume of his cold country – brightly coloured, geometric patterned, heavy cloak (*zeira*), high fawn-skin boots and fox-skin cap with ear flaps. He wore no armour and relied on his speed to get him out of trouble. His weapons were a pair of javelins and a short sword or dagger. Fighting in a loose order formation, his tactic was to run in, throw the javelins and then run away before the enemy could come to grips with him. Unlike the hoplite, he thus emphasizes mobility over shock-power.

These Thracian troops, according to Thucydides (4.28.4), were deployed for the first time in 425 BC by the Athenians at Pylos. Twelve years later, as the Athenians gathered reinforcements for Sicily, 1,300 Thracian peltasts arrived in Athens too late to sail with the relief force headed for Syracuse under Demosthenes (7.27.1). As the Athenians had no wish to incur unnecessary expenditure, they were sent back. But to get some value from the returning peltasts, they appointed one of their own *stratêgoi*, Diitrephes, and 'as they were to sail through the Euipiros, he was instructed to use them in doing whatever damage he could to the enemy on their voyage along the coastline' (7.29.1).

These troops were first used against Tanagra in a quick raid, and then against Mykalessos, both situated in Boiotia. One morning at daybreak the latter town was captured and what followed was one of the worst atrocities of the Peloponnesian War. The Thracians 'butchered the inhabitants sparing neither the young nor the old, but methodically killing everyone they met, women and children alike, and even farm animals and every living thing they saw' (7.29.4). They also stormed a boys' school, 'the largest in the place, into which the children had just entered and killed every one of them' (7.29.5).

There was no honour for the Greeks in fighting from afar. An archer or a javelineer who launched his weapon from a great distance was not held in high esteem, because he could kill with little risk to himself. Only those who clashed with spear and shield, defying death and disdaining retreat, were deemed honourable. Thucydides, describing the first encounter between the Athenians and Syracusans in the autumn of 415 BC, illustrates the relative lack of importance of lightly armed troops in hoplite encounters.

First the stone-throwers, slingers, and archers on both sides engaged each other in front of the main lines of battle, with one party and now another having the advantage, as is normal with these lightly armed troops. (6.69.2)

If would seem that their actions were merely an overture to the actual battle as they could not hope to

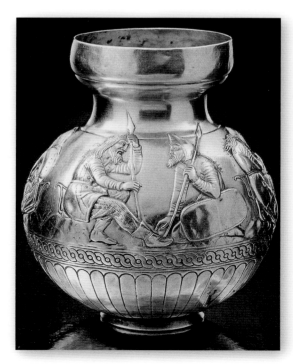

Scythian warriors on a gold vessel (St Petersburg, Hermitage Museum) from the royal tomb at Kul Oba. The *gorytos* (combination quiver-holder and bow-case) of the right-hand warrior is buttoned down, while that of the left is not, thereby revealing his composite bow. (Fields-Carré Collection)

defeat hoplites in pitched battle. However, despite Thucydides' dismissive attitude, if they managed to keep their distance they could wear them down by missile fire, as he says (5.10.9) they did at Amphipolis in 422 BC. As a matter of fact, four years earlier Demosthenes' hoplite force had been severely mauled by swiftly moving Aetolian javelineers, and in the following year he would put his experiences in Aetolia to use by employing a combined force of hoplites and lightly armed men to defeat an isolated, diminutive force of Spartan hoplites at Pylos.

Athenian *stratêgoi* might rely on their oarsmen as makeshift lightly armed troops. This was certainly the case at Pylos when the oarsmen from the top two tiers of each trireme took an active part, 'armed as best they could be' (4.32.2). Indeed, in his letter to the Athenian assembly Nikias commented on the casualties suffered when his sailors were attacked by the enemy cavalry while out 'for fuel, for plunder, and for water' (7.13.2). Oarsmen were bound to arm themselves to the best of their ability, with knives, short swords, slings or javelins.

OPPOSING NAVIES

In the classical period triremes (Greek *triêrês*, Latin *triremis*) were the most formidable (and sophisticated) warships on the Mediterranean. They were galleys, designed to fight under oar power, although two square sails were provided for cruising – a main sail supplied the lift, while a 'boat' sail was used for steering. The excavated ship-sheds at the Peiraieus give us the maximum dimensions for the (Athenian) ships, that is to say, the overall length could not have been more than 40m, and its beam at the widest point no more than 6m.

There is still a great deal of controversy surrounding the trireme but certain factors are clear. It was rowed at three levels with one man to each oar. A chance remark by Thucydides, in which each oarsman of a trireme is said to have 'carried his oar, his cushion and his oar-loop' (2.93.2) from one side of the isthmus to the other, proves there was one man to each oar. We learn from Athenian naval records (the so-called Naval Inventories, e.g. *IG* 2^2 1606.43–44, 1607.14) that these oars were between nine cubits (3.99m) and nine and half cubits (4.2m) long. Of course, because of the nature of our sources, when we talk about navies, we invariably talk about that of Athens.

Oarsmen

'Why is a trireme, fully manned such a terror to the enemy and a joy to her friends', asks Xenophon, 'except by reason of her speed through the water?' (*Oikonomikos* 8.8). In Xenophon's eyes the Athenian trireme's chief virtue was speed, the epitome of efficient muscle power.

In Athens the oarsmen were not slaves but highly trained professionals drawn from the fourth property class as defined by the constitution of the lawgiver Solon (*fl.* 595 BC), the *thêtes*. These men, the poorest Athenian citizens and nicknamed by Aristotle the 'naval mob' (*Politics* 1291b 24, 1304a 22), were renowned for their skills as seamen (Thucydides 1.80.4). Of the *thêtes*, according to the fusty pamphleteer the Old Oligarch, 'the majority can row as soon as they get aboard since they have practised throughout their lives' (Pseudo-Xenophon *Athenaiôn politeia* 1.20). Though written by an opponent of Athens' radical democracy, this is a view that accords well with the words Thucydides puts into the month of Perikles, namely 'sea power is

a matter of skill...and it is not possible to get practice in the odd moment when the chance occurs, but is a full-time occupation, leaving no moment for other things' (1.142.9).

According to the Naval Inventories there were 27 oarsmen each side at the lowest level of the trireme, the *thalamioi*, or hold-rowers. These men worked their oars through oar-ports (*thalamia*). In the middle level there were 27 oarsmen each side, the *zugioi*, or thwart-rowers. The top level of oarsmen, the *thranitai*, or stool-rowers, 31 on each side, rowed through an outrigger (*parexeiresia*). This was an extension beyond the side of the trireme, which gave greater leverage to the oars. The other advantage in this arrangement was the *thranitai* were to one side ('outboard') of those below them, which meant they did not have to be so far above them vertically. This lowered the centre of gravity, making the trireme more stable without increasing its beam. Also, it enabled them to use oars of the same length as those of the other two levels, without having to hold them at a very steep angle to the water. Even so, their task was considered the hardest.

These top-level oarsmen, who as leaders of a 'triad' had a greater responsibility for synchronized rowing, were provided with bonuses on top of their daily wage. According to Thucydides 'the crews of the ships were all paid at the same rate' (3.17.4); before 413 BC this rate was paid at a drachma a day (6.31.3), but halved to three obols in the austere days in the aftermath of the Sicilian expedition (8.45.2). In an effort to keep its crews intact, the Athenian custom was to pay only half the daily rate to the crew while on active service, the rest being due when the ship was paid off in the Peiraieus (8.45.3).

Although the oarsmen were protected to a certain degree from weather and in battle from enemy missiles by a light deck (*katastroma*), the trireme was open at the sides above the topwale. The Syracusans exploited this weakness in the early sea-battles in the Great Harbour, when they employed skiffs to get close in among the Athenian ships and enabled missiles to be thrown in among the oarsmen (7.40.5). There are side-screens (*pararrymata*) of canvas and hide among the gear of triremes in the Naval Inventories (*IG* 2² 1605.40–43, 1609.85-87, 113, 1611.244–249, 1612.73–79, 1627.348). The last were presumably for protection against such attacks, while the first were for protection against the elements. In Xenophon (*Hellenika* 2.1.22, cf. 1.6.19) vertical side-screens are hung over the outriggers just before battle.

It must be said that the *thalamioi* had the most unpleasant and dangerous position. If the ship got badly holed, they were most likely to be drowned or captured by an enemy boarding party. At sea oarsmen were usually unarmed. Also, as Aristophanes (*Frogs* 1074) points out with rather plain vulgarity, they sat with their faces rather close to the backsides of the *zugioi* above and in front of them. They would have suffered also from the sweat of those above dripping down on them. Similarly, their oar-ports were only just above the waterline, and even with efficient *askômata*, they must have become quite wet.

Deck-crew

The full complement of a trireme was 200 (Herodotos 3.13.1–2, 7.184.1, 8.17, Thucydides 6.8.1, 8.29.2, Xenophon *Hellenika* 1.5.3–7), of whom 170 were the oarsmen. According to the Decree of Themistokles (Fornara 55), which apparently records the measures taken by the Athenian assembly in 481 BC to meet the threatened Persian invasion, the fighting men of an Athenian trireme included hoplites enlisted as 'deck-soldiers (*epibatai*), ten to each ship, from men between the ages of 20 and 40, and four archers (*toxotai*)' (lines 23–26).

This left ten deck-hands plus the sea-captain (*triêrarchos*), the helmsman (*kubernêtês*), the bow officer (*prôratês*), the shipwright (*naupêgos*), the boatswain (*keleustês*), who controlled the oarsmen, and a double-pipe player (*aulêtês*), who piped time for them (Anon, *Athenaiôn politeia* 1.2, IG 2² 1951.94–105). Sometimes the oarsmen would join in a rhythmic cry, repeating it over and over, to mark time. The cries O opop, O opop and *ryppapai*, each one mimicking the rhythm of the oar stroke, are both attested for Athenian crews (Aristophanes *Frogs* 208, 1073).

The *kubernêtês* was the highest-ranking professional seaman on a trireme, given that he was in complete charge of navigation under oar and sail. He made decisions, sometimes split-second decisions, which might provide the margin of victory in battle. He was assisted by the *keleustês*, whose business was to manage the oarsmen and get the best out of them (Plato *Alcibiades* 1.125C, Xenophon *Oikonomikos* 21.3). The 14 armed men and the 16 officers and ratings were known collectively as the *hypêresia*, or auxiliary group. They are best seen as assistants to the *triêrarchos*.

Marines

The ten *epibatai* on an Athenian trireme had the highest status in the ship after the *triêrarchos*. They are mentioned second in the Decree of Themistokles and, for instance, at the ceremonial departure of the Sicilian expedition the *epibatai* join their *triêrarchos* in pouring libations (6.32.1).

One reason for the Athenian practice of taking only a few hoplites on deck to serve as marines is due to pulling efficiency. This was seriously jeopardized if there were many people moving about topside and inevitably

The grave stele of Demokleides (Athens, National Archaeological Museum, 752), probably an Athenian, who died at sea serving as an *epibatês*. The pensive young man sits on the foredeck of the trireme in which he served, with his shield and helmet behind him. (Fields-Carré Collection)

caused the ship to roll. Under oar, therefore, the *epibatai* had to be seated (7.67.2), and the procedure appears to have been to keep them centred on the middle line of the ship. When it had come to a stop locked onto an enemy vessel and expecting boarders, the *epibatai* would of course have done no harm by standing up and moving. Thus they would leap up to fight once ships grappled.

Nikias, in his speech before the final sea-battle in the Great Harbour at Syracuse, reveals another reason. Normally the Athenian trireme was built for speed, not strength, and Nikias says:

Many archers and javelineers will be on deck and a mass of hoplites, which we would not employ if we were fighting a battle in the open sea, because they would hinder us through the weight of the ships in exercising our skill. (7.62.2)

Weight, particularly on deck, prevented them doing what they did best, namely bringing off the breakthrough (*diekplous*) and the circling movement (*periplous*), tactical manoeuvres, as we shall see, in which speed and agility were essential.

Finally, the four *toxotai* were distinct from the ten *epibatai*, that is to say, they were not carried on deck. An inscription (*IG* 1^2 950.137), dated to 412/411 BC, gives them a descriptive adjective *paredroi*, 'sitting beside'. It seems that they were posted in the stern beside the *triêrarchos* and *kubernêtês* and acted as their bodyguard in action. The latter would certainly have been vulnerable and would have needed protection, being too busy to defend himself.

Armament

The main weapon of a trireme was the bronze-plated ram (*embolos*) situated at the prow. Aischylos speaks of the use of 'brazen rams' (*Persai* 408, 415) at Salamis, and they appear in the Naval Inventories as returnable items when a ship is broken up (*IG* 2^2 1623.113–123, 1628.498). The ram was formed by the forward tip of the keel, heavily armoured and built up to a point with three chisel-like blades just above water level. The join between the ram and the sternpost, which curved upwards and forwards, was shaped to reduce water resistance so that the whole structure acted both as an armament and as a cutwater.

Before the invention of gunpowder, and long after, the offensive capabilities of warships were limited to setting an enemy vessel on fire, or piercing the hull at the waterline, or by boarding. Advances in Greek warship design were aimed at achieving the speed necessary for successful ramming without loss of stability. Impact theory indicates that unless the attacker reached the critical speed of about ten knots at the moment of impact, it would crumple, while the target vessel escaped almost unscathed. The oarsmen obviously needed to deliver a high strike rate, perhaps approaching

50 strokes per minute (Shaw 1993: 100). Ominously the Greek word for stroke, *embolê*, is the same word used for 'charge' or 'ramming'.

The ram could smash a hole in an enemy vessel and so cripple her, but could not literally sink her. Ancient sources use terms meaning 'sink', but it is evident that ships so 'sunk' could still be towed away. For instance, the Greek word *kataduein*, which is almost invariably translated as 'sink', in fact means no more than 'dip' or 'lower'. So, when triremes were holed in a sea-battle, though they had become absolutely useless as fighting vessels, the combatants went to great lengths and some risk to recover the wrecks. These could be towed home as prizes; after being repaired, equipped and re-named, they became part of the navy (*IG* 2² 1606).

Tactics

Lack of space in the hull for food and water, low freeboard, low cruising speed under oars, and limited sailing qualities lowered the trireme's range of operations. Thus, in addition to the necessity for regular beaching to allow the crews to eat and sleep, naval engagements customarily took place near the coast, where ships could be handled in relatively calm water and there was some hope for the shipwrecked. Sails were used for fleets in transit, but when approaching the battle area the masts would be lowered and the ships rowed. The opposing fleets normally deployed in line abreast two deep.

There were two main methods of fighting, which placed contradictory demands on trireme design. The first was ramming. This called for the smallest possible ship built around the largest number of rowers. The Athenian navy with its small number of marines followed this philosophy. The other was boarding. This called for larger, heavier ships able to carry the maximum number of boarders. The Chiots, for example, with their 40 marines per trireme (Herodotos 6.15.2), followed this philosophy. The latter view eventually prevailed, since, to ram, a vessel had to make contact, which was just what the boarders wanted. Hence the later development of large ships with full decks (triremes were only partially decked), namely the four, five and six-banked ships of the Hellenistic period, which were primarily designed as heavily armoured floating platforms to carry either catapults or marines.

In his scornful description of the sea-battle of Sybota (433 BC), Thucydides says the style of fighting had been 'of the old clumsy sort' (1.49.1). Here the triremes were carrying many hoplites and archers and the engagement 'had almost the appearance of a battle by land' (*pezomachia*, 1.49.2) with both sides (apart from the small Athenian contingent) fighting 'with fury and brute strength rather than with skill' (1.49.3). Thucydides' so-called old-fashioned style of fighting was obviously a reliance on sea-soldiers of various sorts topside, either repelling boarders or themselves boarding another vessel.

Whether boarding or ramming, ships had to collide, and this also limited their tactical capabilities. With the ram the trireme itself could be used as an offensive weapon, but the problem was to avoid damaging one's own ship or becoming so entangled with the enemy vessel that boarding became inevitable. Yet speed and manoeuvrability could make it possible to attack vulnerable sides and sterns. For the Athenians, ramming head-on had come to be considered a sign of lack of skill in a helmsman (7.36.5), and the manoeuvre-and-ram school, in which the Athenian navy reigned supreme, relied on two tactical options, the *diekplous* and the *periplous*.

The ram was designed to cause maximum waterline damage without penetrating the hull too far and making it difficult for the attacking vessel to disengage. In *Olympias*, the full-scale replica of Morrison and Coates, the bronze sheath weighs some 200kg. (Fields-Carré Collection)

Diekplous and periplous

The *diekplous* was a manoeuvre involving single ships in line abeam, the standard battle formation, in which each helmsman would steer for a gap in the enemy line. He would then either turn suddenly to port or starboard to ram an enemy ship in the side or row clean through the line, swing round and smash into the stern of an enemy ship. The top-deck would be lined with marines and archers at the ready, but their main role was mainly defensive. The main weapon was the attacking ship's ram.

Neither Herodotos, Thucydides nor Xenophon make the details of this manoeuvre very clear, but Polybios, in his account of the sea-battle of Drepana (249 BC), describes it as such: 'To sail through the enemy's line and to appear from behind, while they were already fighting others [in front], which is a most effective naval manoeuvre' (1.51.8). Although he is writing in the second century BC about a naval engagement that was fought in the third century BC, the action was still contested by ships propelled by oars and armed with rams. Moreover, the Carthaginian ships executing this 'most effective naval manoeuvre' were well constructed and had experienced oarsmen.

The *periplous* was either a variation involving outflanking the enemy line when there was plenty of sea room, or the final stage of the *diekplous*, when the manoeuvring vessel, having cut through the line, swung round to attack from the stern. Once the enemy formation had broken up the *periplous* would have become the most important tactical option available to the helmsman (Thucydides 7.36.3, 4, Xenophon *Hellenika* 1.6.31).

And so the *periplous* was a tactical manoeuvre that a single, skilfully handled vessel performed to make a ramming attack that did not involve prow-to-prow contact. Even so, it required room for its execution, and timing was of the essence. With a modest speed of nine knots each trireme, assailant and victim, would travel its own length in about six and a half seconds. If the attacker arrived too soon, he could himself be struck and holed by the target vessel, too late and the speed of impact fell off rapidly and he could deliver no more than a mild bump.

Since both manoeuvres required plenty of sea room, there were two countermoves to the *diekplous* and *periplous*: first, to occupy a position that was crowded – this was the case, as we shall discover, with regards to the four sea-battles in the Great Harbour of Syracuse; or, if in open water, form the *kuklos*, a defensive circle with rams pointing outwards (2.83.5, 3.78.1). The alternative, especially for a large fleet, was to form up in double line abeam (Xenophon *Hellenika* 1.6.28). The ships in the second line would try and pick off any enemy vessel that broke through before it could turn and ram a friendly vessel in the first line.

OPPOSING PLANS

The Athenians had a long-standing interest in the far west. Besides involvement in establishing the colony of Thourioi (444/443 BC), the Athenians had entered into alliances with various Greek and non-Greek states of southern Italy and Sicily. For the most part, these alliances were the usual offensive and defensive treaty (*symmachia*) whose basic term was the agreement between the contracting parties 'to have the same friends and enemies'. This was presumably out of a desire to exert some influence in this important grain-producing area, but probably not in any expectation that it would come under their direct hegemony – hence the alliance with Corcyra (433 BC) on the grounds (among others) that it 'lay very conveniently on the coastal route to Italy and Sicily' (1.44.3). However, during the Peloponnesian War we see the desire for influence turning into a desire for conquest, and a consequent feeling that such conquest was a real possibility, especially after the 'failure' of 427–424 BC when the Athenians had first intervened militarily in Sicily.

Having responded to an appeal for help from their Ionian kinsmen and allies of Leontinoi, who were at war with the Syracusans, the mood of the Athenians had swung decisively in favour of conquest as the desired means to end the campaign in Sicily. Hence the three *stratêgoi*, Eurymedon among them, were penalized for failing to bring home a victory for which they had

The Porto Piccolo, looking south-west towards Ortygia. Originally a bay of the Great Harbour, it was here that the Syracusans had their old dockyards. These were protected during the siege with a palisade constructed from massive stakes driven into the seabed. (Fields-Carré Collection)

never been equipped. If an opportunity were to present itself in the future, conquest would be the only satisfactory outcome for the majority of the Athenians. In 416 BC Egesta (the Latin form of the name is Segesta) was being hard pressed by Selinous (Selinunte) and Syracuse, and called upon the Athenians to come to their aid by sending a fleet.

Egesta was not numbered among the Greek colonies of Sicily but was in fact one of the principal centres of the Elymians, the indigenous inhabitants of the western part of the island. However, the Egestaians had assimilated many of the material aspects of Greek culture, even making a formal agreement on intermarriage with their Greek neighbours at Selinous. It seems that it was this particular issue that was the cause of their quarrel with Selinous and its protector, Syracuse. Thucydides (6.2.3) records a tradition that the Elymians were descendants of refugees from Troy, perhaps led by the great Trojan hero Aeneas himself, as Virgil maintained (*Aeneid* 4.710-719).

THE ATHENIAN PLAN

Euripides' *Trojan Women* was produced in 415 BC, right after the Athenian slaughter of the Melians and on the eve of the grand expedition to Sicily. The Athenian tragedian has Kassandra condemn the Greek attack on Troy on a variety of moral grounds, and her caustic indictment makes little effort to mask Euripides' own obvious disgust with Athenian *hubris*: those who have the power do what they will, those who do not, do what they must.

In our main source too, the *History of the Peloponnesian War* by Euripides' contemporary Thucydides, the Sicilian expedition is presented as an act of folly by an arrogant, imperial power. At the opening of the sixth book, he implies that Sicily was too large to conquer, and he presents the decision to sail to the far west as an act of irrational exuberance. All the same, with the Peloponnesian War in a state of uneasy truce, Athens, ostensibly to preserve the independence of its allies Egesta and Leontinoi, launched an expedition to capture Syracuse.

At the very start of the Peloponnesian War, Perikles, according to Thucydides, had advised the Athenians not 'to add to the empire during the course of the war' (2.65.7). For Thucydides, who greatly admired Perikles, the Sicilian expedition was a prime example of the Athenian people being misled by their emotions. Yet the initial plan of dispatching a small naval expedition to Sicily was not a bad one, and Athens was morally obliged to support its western allies against Syracuse and its allies. Thucydides says Nikias was unwilling to be one of the three *stratêgoi*, believing 'the city was making a mistake and, on a slight pretext, which looked reasonable, was in fact aiming at conquering the whole of Sicily' (6.8.4), and he speaks to the assembly to air his objections. But after a response from Alcibiades, he says 'the Athenians became more eager than before to make the expedition' (6.19.1).

Nikias then changed tack, saying he wanted much more than the 60 triremes agreed upon. But his clumsy attempt to dampen their enthusiasm by putting requirements unacceptably high backfired. Eventually someone came forwards and addressed Nikias personally, telling him not to beat about the bush but 'to let him now say in front of everyone what forces the Athenians were to vote for him' (6.25.1). After he had reluctantly done so, they 'immediately voted that the *stratêgoi* should have full powers with regard to the numbers of the army and to the expedition in general' (6.26.1).

And so a modest operation was converted into an elephantine expedition, which now meant the Athenian western allies started to suspect that the armada was not just there to help them, but had other objectives. Worse still, if something went wrong, Athens would have no forces left and would be defenceless against Sparta. Yet Nikias was not the only one who is to blame for the ultimate disaster. Some Athenians, chief among them Alcibiades, wanted even bigger things, like an attack on Carthage. For the time being, however, the official plan was to support the allies only, and the unstated aim was to conquer the island.

For Alcibiades, or so Plutarch claims, Sicily was just the beginning of a campaign of conquest that would encompass Carthage, Libya, Italy, and then the Peloponnese. In Plutarch's account this grandiose plan certainly gripped the imagination of the Athenians: young and old alike sat in the gymnasia and other public places 'sketching in the sand the outline of Sicily and the position of Carthage and Libya' (*Alcibiades* 17.6). Thucydides (6.90.2–3) gives a different order to the projected campaign in a speech he puts in the mouth of Alcibiades after his defection to the Spartans: first Sicily, then the Greeks of Italy, after them the Carthaginians, and then, with the overwhelming resources of the far west, to crush the Peloponnese. Was this grand strategy, or mere fantasy?

The evidence of Plutarch can be considered to derive from Thucydides, and thus to have no independent value with regards to the true nature of Athenian ambitions in the far west. From Thucydides, however, passages can be used to argue for and against the reality of the plan. It is most fully explained in the speech of Alcibiades that seeks to persuade the Spartans to renew the war against Athens (6.90). Here, there is every reason for Alcibiades to exaggerate before his no-doubt suspicious hosts. It is clear that a so-called grand plan was not raised openly in the assembly meeting that discussed sending the enlarged expedition (6.9–14, 16–18, 20–23), or in the war council of the *stratêgoi* when they reached Sicily (6.48). From Sicily the Athenians actually asked the Carthaginians for aid (6.88.6). On the other hand, it was Thucydides' own opinion that the Athenians desired all Sicily (6.1.1, 6.1) and that Alcibiades aimed at Carthage (6.15.2). Any attempt on Sicily automatically would have caused conflict with Carthage, which controlled the western half of the island. The fact that the Athenians were receiving aid from the Etruscans of central Italy (6.103.2) indicates the wide scale of their involvement in the western Mediterranean. In a speech Thucydides gives to Hermokrates, the Carthaginians are said to be constantly apprehensive that they will one day be attacked by the Athenians (6.34.2).

Already in a comedy produced in 424 BC, the possibility of an Athenian attack on Carthage had been mentioned, albeit with a creative exaggeration (Aristophanes *Knights* 1302–1305). It was not openly acknowledged policy, but the idea was certainly in the air. Had the Athenian expedition met with more success in Sicily, the 'grand plan' may well have appeared attractive.

Cicero's *forum amplissiimum*, on Foro Siracusano. Located on an east–west road that terminated at the Great Harbour, the Roman forum corresponded to the agora of the Greek city. As quaestor of Sicily (75–74 BC), Cicero knew Syracuse very well. (Fields-Carré Collection)

THE SYRACUSAN PLAN

Thucydides interrupts his narrative of the preparations for the Sicilian expedition with an account of a debate at Syracuse about the prospects of invasion. One of the speakers, Hermokrates, puts forward an idea to deter the invading force before it reaches Italy. He suggests the dispatch of a Syracusan fleet with two months' victuals to Taras. 'They have a great stretch of open sea to cross with their expeditionary force', he says, 'and because of the length of the voyage it will be difficult for this force to keep its order, but easy for us to attack it as it comes up slowly and in detachments' (6.34.3). Hermokrates fully appreciated the operational limitations of the trireme, but despite the logic of his arguments the Syracusans were not convinced of the urgency to adopt his plan.

The size and competence of the Syracusan navy at this time is something of a mystery. In Thucydides' view it was, of course, untrained and inexperienced in comparison with the Athenian navy, and the gradual reversal of roles is a major theme of the seventh book of his work. Diodoros (12.30.1), himself a Siciliote Greek, records the construction of 100 triremes at Syracuse in 439/438 BC, and though this is belied by the ease with which 20 Athenian ships operated in Sicilian waters between 427 BC and 425 BC, the Syracusans had at least 80 triremes by the summer of 413 BC (7.22.1).

Still, whatever the competence of their navy, the Athenian lack of urgency meant the Syracusans were to be given four months in which to rectify any weaknesses. Prompted by Hermokrates, they slimmed down their command structure – they had fielded no fewer than 15 *stratêgoi* at the battle of the Anapos – and introduced a vigorous training programme for their inexperienced hoplites, an unusual measure among the amateur citizen-militias of the Greeks. Another unusual measure was to give arms to poorer men to enable them to fight as hoplites. In addition, they decided to enlarge the line of fortifications so that any future circumvallation would have to be much longer. They also sent envoys to Corinth and Sparta asking for direct assistance. Another winter success for Hermokrates was thwarting the Athenians' attempt to secure help from Kamarina.

In the spring of 414 BC, therefore, the Athenians were to lay siege to a Syracuse that had been prepared by Hermokrates, who was now one of the three newly elected *stratêgoi* granted full powers to make decisions without consulting the Syracusan assembly. The most important preparation was that the mainland part of the city had been reinforced with a new fortification wall. Taking in the ground of Apollo Temenites, the 'winter wall' ran south to north across Epipolai, to reach the sea near Trogilos. Thus, the area that had to be covered by any future Athenian siege works was substantially increased. The Syracusans also planted forts at the Olympieion, adjacent to the earlier battlefield, and at Megara Hyblaia, 'and stuck stakes into the sea at all the possible landing places' (6.75.1). Megara Hyblaia, some 14km north of Syracuse, was in fact deserted, its inhabitants having been driven out by the tyrant Gelon some 60 years previously.

THE TARGET

Syracuse had been founded in the third quarter of the 8th century BC on the long, narrow island of Ortygia (Quail Island), which was nearly attached to the mainland at its northern edge. As what came to be known as the inner city grew, it had spread onto the adjacent mainland to form the outer city. Here a massive limestone outcrop, Achradina, butted into the sea, with its western edge leading onto the lower slopes of Epipolai ('Over-city'), the vast limestone plateau, more or less triangular in shape, which dominated the city to the north-west. In the middle of the 6th century BC, Ortygia was linked to the

A colonnade of a Doric-style temple, assimilated into the north wall of the Duomo, looking south-east on Via Minerva in Syracuse. Dedicated to Athena, the temple was built by Gelon to celebrate the victory over the Carthaginians at Himera in 480 BC. (Fields-Carré Collection)

mainland by a causeway. Despite its growth, however, at the time of the siege the nucleus of Syracuse remained Ortygia – easily defensible, with harbours to the north and south, and a good source of water, the fountain of Arethusa.

Ortygia partly closed a deep bay, the Great Harbour – an impressive sheet of water some 3.5km from north to south. The entrance to the bay, from the southern tip of Ortygia to the headland of Plemmyrion opposite, was just over a kilometre wide. The inner city was defended by a circuit wall that probably ran from somewhere on the north-east shore of the Great Harbour to the sea coast, to include the Little Harbour, the military port of Syracuse, which was tucked into a bay between the northern end of Ortygia and the mainland.

However, the physical aspect of this area is considerably different today. The accumulation of silt washed up by the current into the Great Harbour has resulted in an advancing coastline on the west side of Ortygia, while a concurrent advance of the sea on the east side of Ortygia has resulted in the total disappearance of the Little Harbour. The perimeter of the latter, bounded on the north and south by two promontories, has completely submerged, while the inner area of the present Porto Piccolo was formerly part of the ancient Great Harbour. Just to the east of this was the ancient causeway, and on this was what Cicero called the 'narrow bridge', the continuation north of the main road that skirted the three main temples of Ortygia and linked the island to the mainland.

The fountain of Arethusa, the mythical spring celebrated by Pindar and Virgil, was the symbol of Syracuse from its foundation. When Arethusa was bathing in the Alpheios near Olympia, so legend has it, the river god fell in love with her. To escape from him she plunged into the sea and resurfaced in Syracuse, only to be turned into a spring by Artemis. Nevertheless, Alpheios, in hot pursuit, mingled his waters with that of the spring. In ancient times it was believed that this Peloponnesian river was connected, via the Ionian Sea, to the Sicilian spring, but in actual fact, it is one of the many openings of the Hyblaean phreatic fold, the same one that feeds the Anapos river. The Anapos (Fiume Anapo) still flows into the Great Harbour on the west, and south of the river, on high ground some 1.6km from the (modern) shore, was the Olympieion, a sanctuary of Olympian Zeus. Near the temple was a small settlement.

THE CAMPAIGN

The Athenians had a formidable line-up of alliances in both Italy and Sicily. In Italy, Greek states on the Athenian side included Rhegion, Metapontion, Thourioi, and those of Campania. In Sicily the Athenians' initial friends included Leontinoi, Kamarina, Katana, and finally, most importantly, and most controversially, non-Greek Egesta, far over in the west of the island. The evidence for the alliance of Athens and Egesta is an inscription (Fornara 81) whose date is disputed. The traditional date is 458/457 BC, but it is now claimed that new computerized techniques of laser enhancement indicate a much later date for the inscription, namely 418/417 BC, which is surprising, though not incredible, as Thucydides makes no mention of it.

In both regions the Athenians had friends among the native peoples hostile to the local Greek population. Thus in Italy there was the friendship of the Messapian Iapygii in the hinterland of Sparta's colony Taras, and the Etruscans much farther to the north of the peninsula, and in Sicily the friendship of the Sikels, who inhabited the eastern and central parts of the island.

With the fleet's arrival in Italy, however, the Athenians' supposed friends the Rhegines, allowed them to drag their ships ashore and camp on some sacred ground where a small market was set up for them, but refused to admit them to their city. And generally the Athenians had a serious problem about the neutrality of the Siciliote and Italiote Greeks. The wealthy and powerful *polis* of Akragas (Agrigento) was the most notable of these and took no part in the war (7.33.2, 58.1). But in Rhegion's case the reason for the frigid reception of the Athenians may be that they were simply intimidated by the scale of their armament as it appeared over the horizon. It was all very well to make alliances with distant Athens, but this looked alarmingly like a conquering fleet. 'When they see us exhausted, they will come here one day with larger forces and will attempt to bring all of us under their control' (4.60.2), or so Hermokrates had warned his fellow delegates nine years previously at the Gela peace conference.

THE ATHENIAN ARMADA

The armada included 134 triremes in all, of which 100 were Athenian, the rest from Chios and other allies. Sixty of the Athenian triremes were 'fast' (*tacheiai*) that is, fighting triremes, the rest 'troopships' (*stratiôtides*). The latter differed structurally to some extent, and were rowed by the soldiers they carried, supervised by a skeleton crew of experienced sailors. But it is almost certain that they could be used as fighting ships, though this would involve some modification.

The routes of the Athenian armada, Gylippos, Corinthians and Athenian reinforcements, 415–413 BC

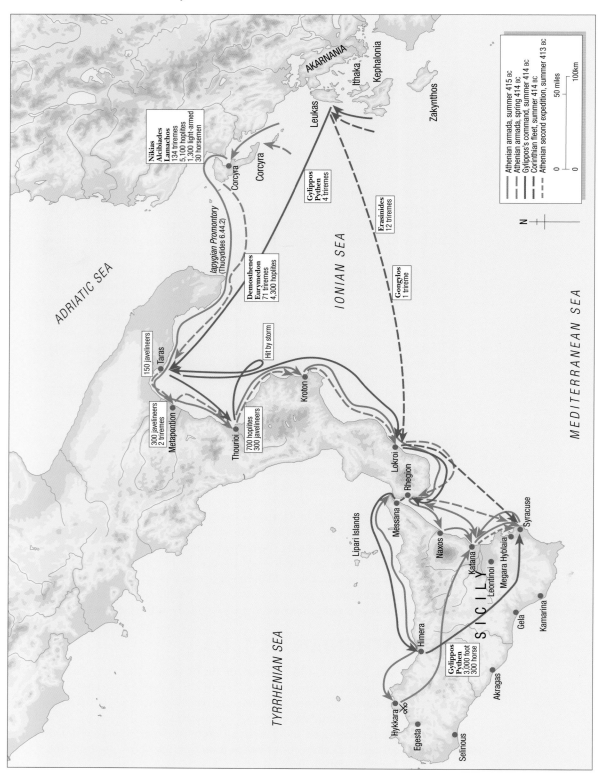

Nikias
Alcibiades
Lamachos
134 triremes
5,100 hoplites
1,300 light-armed
30 horsemen

Gylippos
Pythen
4 triremes

Erasinides
12 triremes

Gongylos
1 trireme

Iapygian Promontory
(Thucydides 6.44.2)

Demosthenes
Eurymedon
71 triremes
4,300 hoplites

Hit by storm

150 javelineers
Taras

300 javelineers
2 triremes
Metapontion

700 hoplites
300 javelineers
Thourioi

Kroton

AKARNANIA

Leukas

Corcyra

Corcyra

Ithaka

Kephalonia

Zakynthos

ADRIATIC SEA

IONIAN SEA

MEDITERRANEAN SEA

TYRRHENIAN SEA

Lokroi

Rhegion

Messana

Lipari Islands

Naxos

Katana

Leontinoi

Megara Hyblaia

Syracuse

S I C I L Y

Gylippos
Pythen
3,000 foot
300 horse

Himera

Gela

Kamarina

Akragas

Hykkara

Egesta

Selinous

Athenian armada, summer 415 BC
Athenian armada, spring 414 BC
Gylippos's command, summer 414 BC
Corinthian fleet, summer 414 BC
Athenian second expedition, summer 413 BC

0   50 miles
0   100km

N

The troops consisted of 5,100 hoplites, 1,500 of them Athenian, with lightly armed troops in proportion. These included 700 Rhodian slingers and 480 archers, of whom 80 were Cretan specialists and the rest Athenians (and Scythians) originally serving on the triremes as *toxotai*. Athens also supplied 700 *thêtes*, who normally shipped as citizen-oarsmen, equipped as hoplites so as to serve as marines on the fighting triremes. These men from the lowest property class, who could not afford to pay for hoplite panoply, were given arms at state expense. The rest of the hoplites were allied troops, some of whom were subjects of Athens, though there were also 500 Argives and 250 Mantineians as well as other mercenaries. Ominously, one horse-transport (*hippagôgos*), a converted trireme, carried 30 men and their mounts, the only cavalry on the expedition (6.43).

Essential supplies were carried by 30 merchantmen, which also transported bakers, stonemasons and carpenters, and the tools for building fortifications. A hundred smaller craft had been requisitioned, like the merchantmen, and many other vessels voluntarily followed the armada in order to trade (6.44.1).

Though the bulk of the triremes, as always, were Athenian, the crews appear mainly to have been drawn from non-Athenians. This was hardly surprising when we consider the sheer number of sailors required to crew such an enterprise – 10,200 oarsmen needed for the 60 fighting triremes alone. A decree concerned with the preparations for the initial expedition has been restored, to provide for the recruiting of volunteers from the cities of the empire (Fornara 146), and before Thucydides begins his dramatic account of the fourth and final sea-battle in the Great Harbour of Syracuse, he takes the opportunity to enhance its climatic status by saying 'there had certainly never been so many peoples gathered together in front of a single city' (7.56.4). Somewhat reminiscent of Homer, he then proceeds to present a catalogue of the allies of Athens (and Syracuse), recounting their ethnicity, their status, and the circumstances that led to them being there. Again, when Thucydides

The Fountain of Arethusa, looking north from Porto Grande in Syracuse. The spring of the water nymph Arethusa, once lauded by poets, now flows into a pond under the ficus tree. Nelson apparently watered his fleet here before the battle of the Nile. (Fields-Carré Collection)

has Nikias address the sailors before they embark, he implies that the majority were not Athenian. Many of these would have been *metoikoi*, foreigners resident in Athens, men 'regarded as Athenians, although they are not, because they know our dialect and imitate our ways' (7.63.3).

ARRIVAL IN SICILY

On arrival in Sicily the dismay of the Athenians only increased. Learning that the financial resources of the Egestaians proved to be illusory – only 30 of the promised 60 talents were available but as yet not delivered – the three Athenian *stratêgoi* took counsel together. Lamachos, who was chosen as *stratêgos* purely and simply on the basis of his soldierly skills, proposed an immediate all-out attack on Syracuse, and Thucydides says (6.49, cf. 7.42.3) taking the city when it was still unprepared and in a state of alarm would have been the best course of action. Nikias, however, recommended that the Athenians merely show the flag, preferring to bring about some sort of settlement between Egesta and Selinous, and then, after sailing around the island in a display of strength, return home, taking no further risks unless the opportunity arose to help Leontinoi or win over other allies. Then again, Alcibiades proposed instead that they should find more allies, establish a base of operations, and attack Syracuse only after this build-up. In the end, his plan was adopted and Katana, a little to the north of Syracuse, became the Athenian base.

Yet the crucial element of surprise was lost, and from the outset the Athenians were to suffer from command problems. Alcibiades, summoned home to stand trial for his alleged part in the Herms and Mysteries scandal, absconded to Sparta, leaving two commanders in charge who did not agree with the strategy they had embarked upon. Even worse, the able Lamachos was destined to fall during the early stages of the siege. This would thus leave Nikias in sole command of a massive and aggressive campaign he himself had advised against from its inception.

THE PHONEY WAR

With Alcibiades gone, the whole fleet sailed north from Katana through the straits of Messina and west along the north coast of Sicily. According to Thucydides (6.62.1), the intention was to see whether the Egestaians could provide the promised funds, and to look to the differences between them and the Selinountines, which is exactly what Nikias had proposed in the first place. They put in first at Himera, where they were refused admittance, and then took Hykkara (Carini), a native town on the coast at war with Egesta. The town was handed over to the Egestaians, whose cavalry had come to help, but its inhabitants were shipped back to Katana where they were sold. The Athenian army then marched back to Katana through friendly Sikel territory. Nikias himself, meanwhile, made his way to Egesta 'and, after receiving 30 talents and doing some other business, rejoined the rest of the expedition' (6.62.4). The 'other business' was, presumably, a failed attempt to patch up the differences between the Egestaians and the Selinountines.

Nikias' next move appears to suggest that he had decided at last to adopt the strategy of his colleague, Lamachos. Using a false promise of betrayal by a Katanaian double agent, Nikias lured the whole Syracusan army to Katana, while the Athenian forces sailed around to the Great Harbour in Syracuse. Nikias might have attempted at this moment to seize the city by assault, as he had the whole Athenian army outside Syracuse, whose army in turn was by now outside Katana, but he decided to await its return. The Syracusans returned speedily to find the enemy drawn up in an excellent position near the Anapos river. On the next morning, the Athenians advanced to attack,

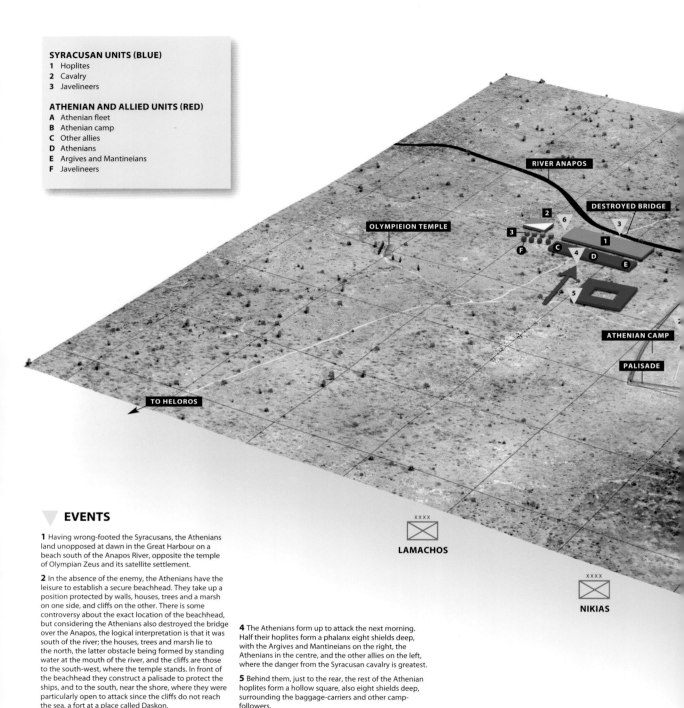

SYRACUSAN UNITS (BLUE)
1 Hoplites
2 Cavalry
3 Javelineers

ATHENIAN AND ALLIED UNITS (RED)
A Athenian fleet
B Athenian camp
C Other allies
D Athenians
E Argives and Mantineians
F Javelineers

RIVER ANAPOS

DESTROYED BRIDGE

OLYMPIEION TEMPLE

ATHENIAN CAMP

PALISADE

TO HELOROS

xxxx
LAMACHOS

xxxx
NIKIAS

▼ EVENTS

1 Having wrong-footed the Syracusans, the Athenians land unopposed at dawn in the Great Harbour on a beach south of the Anapos River, opposite the temple of Olympian Zeus and its satellite settlement.

2 In the absence of the enemy, the Athenians have the leisure to establish a secure beachhead. They take up a position protected by walls, houses, trees and a marsh on one side, and cliffs on the other. There is some controversy about the exact location of the beachhead, but considering the Athenians also destroyed the bridge over the Anapos, the logical interpretation is that it was south of the river; the houses, trees and marsh lie to the north, the latter obstacle being formed by standing water at the mouth of the river, and the cliffs are those to the south-west, where the temple stands. In front of the beachhead they construct a palisade to protect the ships, and to the south, near the shore, where they were particularly open to attack since the cliffs do not reach the sea, a fort at a place called Daskon.

3 When the duped Syracusan army finally arrives to find the Athenians firmly entrenched outside their city, they challenge them to fight. But the Athenians refuse to rise to the bait, and the Syracusans can do nothing but make camp for the night.

4 The Athenians form up to attack the next morning. Half their hoplites form a phalanx eight shields deep, with the Argives and Mantineians on the right, the Athenians in the centre, and the other allies on the left, where the danger from the Syracusan cavalry is greatest.

5 Behind them, just to the rear, the rest of the Athenian hoplites form a hollow square, also eight shields deep, surrounding the baggage-carriers and other camp-followers.

6 The Syracusans, meanwhile, deploy their inexperienced hoplites 16 shields deep, their cavalry and javelineers posted on the right of this deeply formed phalanx. As storm clouds gather overhead, the Athenian main line-of-battle advances and takes the enemy by surprise.

THE BATTLE OF THE ANAPOS, AUTUMN 415 BC

The Syracusans, having returned from Katana, clash with the main body of the Athenian force at the Anapos River, to the south of Syracuse. The Athenians catch them off guard, and win an emphatic victory.

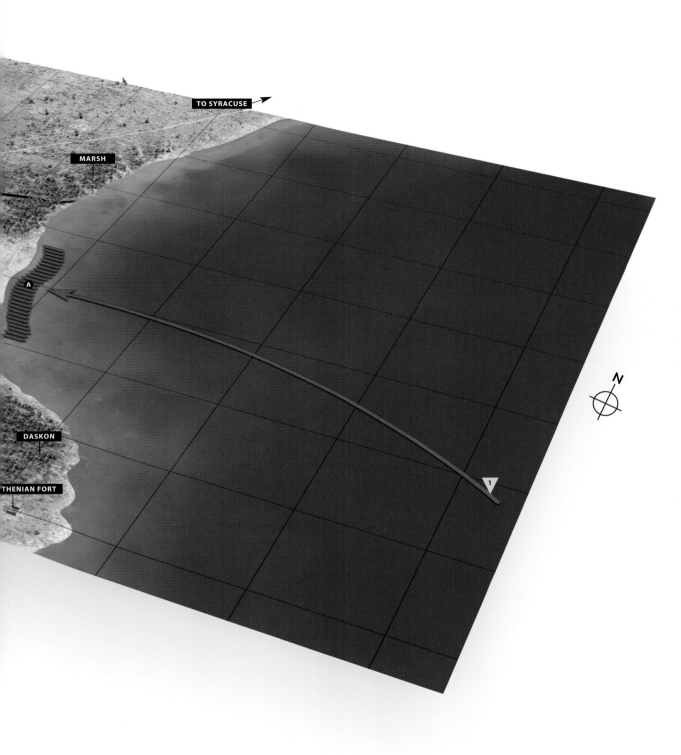

TO SYRACUSE

MARSH

A

DASKON

THENIAN FORT

N

1

TOP

A view from the Olympieion looking east-north-east towards Ortygia and the Great Harbour. It was on this ground south of the Anapos that the first encounter took place between the Athenians and Syracusans. The Athenian palisade was somewhere near the shore. (Fields-Carré Collection)

CENTRE

The mouth of the Anapos, looking east from Via Elorina bridge. The Athenians landed just to the south and, as part of their pre-battle preparations, they broke down the bridge over the river. Note the pill-box left over from World War II. (Fields-Carré Collection)

BOTTOM

Punta Caderini, the wooded promontory Thucydides (6.66.2) calls Daskon. It was here that the Athenians, on the eve of the battle of the Anapos, threw up a temporary fort of stones and timber to protect the southern flank of their beachhead. (Fields-Carré Collection)

catching the Syracusans off guard, and won a resounding victory by exploiting the Syracusans' lack of combat experience. Having erected a trophy on the battlefield, the Athenians immediately set sail for Katana and their winter quarters.

THE SIEGE BEGINS

The following spring, with 650 cavalry from Athens, Egesta and the Sikels, Nikias and Lamachos initiated their strategy of close-drawn circumvallation to capture Syracuse. This involved the seizure of the rocky heights, known as Epipolai, overlooking the city. Flat-topped and three-sided, Epipolai stretches from its eastern end, roughly the area enclosed by the Syracusan 'winter wall', and rises to its highest point (188m), modern Belvedere, in the west. Near to its apex is Euryelos ('Large Nail'), a point where the plateau is still high (140m) and narrows to form a 'waist'; the north and the south sides of the triangle consist of steep cliffs, and the easiest ascent to the plateau is at Euryelos. The Syracusans, therefore, 'thought that, unless the Athenians could control Epipolai they would find it difficult, even if victorious in battle, to build a wall to cut the city off' (6.96.1). But they were too late.

Nikias and Lamachos landed the army at Leon before daybreak, marched at speed to Epipolai and seized control of Euryelos, easily defeating the 600 Syracusan hoplites picked to guard it. Meanwhile, the fleet came to anchor at Thapsos (Penisola Magnisi), a narrow-necked peninsula that juts into the sea just north of Leon. Here the sailors began erecting a stockade across the isthmus. Lazenby (2004: 146), pointing out the stark contrast between the Athenians' strategic ineptitude and their tactical expertise, makes the interesting suggestion that perhaps Nikias was responsible for the strategy but left its tactical implementation to Lamachos.

The following day the Athenian army severed Syracuse's land communications with two forts. One was erected at Labdalon on the steep ground somewhere along the northern cliffs looking towards Megara Hyblaia, and it was here they stored their supplies, equipment and war chest (6.97.5). The other fort was planted at Syke ('Fig Tree') just west of Achradina and not far from the southern cliffs of Epipolai, and it was protected by an outwork to the east. Syke was possibly a well-known landmark, and Thucydides calls the fort there 'the Circle' (6.98.2), and it was to serve as the hub of operations for the Athenians while they conducted the siege. Thucydides says the Syracusans were dismayed by the speed of these operations, and decided to give battle. But with the two armies already facing each other, the Syracusan *stratêgoi* saw their men were not properly in line and withdrew to the city, leaving part of their cavalry to harass the building operations.

A strange war of walling and counter-walling began. The Athenians knew that they had to hem in the Syracusans so they could starve them into submission. They started their circumvallation from the Circle, northwards in the direction of Trogilos, close to where the army had landed, and southwards towards the Great Harbour: sea to harbour measured some 3.5km. The Syracusans' main defence was to construct a counter-wall that would run in a westerly direction from the 'winter wall' to cut across the intended line of the Athenian wall of circumvallation. Consisting of a stockade, the counter-wall was begun from a position roughly opposite the Circle and stretched to the southern escarpment of Epipolai. However, Syracusan negligence and Athenian daring resulted in the capture and

RIGHT

Euryelos, looking north-west from Mura Dionigiane. Though high at this point (140m), Euryelos is a naturally easy route of access onto Epipolai. Begun by Dionysios (402 BC), a fortress (Castello Eurialo) was built to command the western approaches to Syracuse. (Fields-Carré Collection)

BELOW, RIGHT

A track winding up the northern cliffs of Epipolai, looking east towards Targia. Having landed at Leon, the Athenian army made its way at the double on to Epipolai by way of Euryelos. Ancient Leon lies somewhere on the left of this snapshot. (Fields-Carré Collection)

destruction of the counter-wall and further progress for the Athenian circumvallation south of the Circle. In order to protect their ships, the wall was made double on the lower ground between the cliffs of Epipolai and the Great Harbour.

The rate with which this double wall was being erected greatly alarmed the Syracusans. They responded by building a second counter-wall, another stockade but this time with a ditch running beside it, through the marshy area below the southern cliffs of Epipolai, so that they could at least retain command of a road to the inland of Sicily. By placing planks and doors on the firmest parts of the marsh, a picked body of Athenians, led by the bold Lamachos, destroyed the stockade, but was unable to prevent an attack on the Circle, which could only be saved by Nikias ordering the baggage-carriers to set fire to its supplies of timber. The siege machinery was also destroyed. Worse, Lamachos was killed, quite suddenly (6.101.6). The cautious Nikias, who was by now suffering from a diseased kidney, was left in the unenviable position of sole command.

Syracuse, Epipolai and the key battles, 414–413 BC

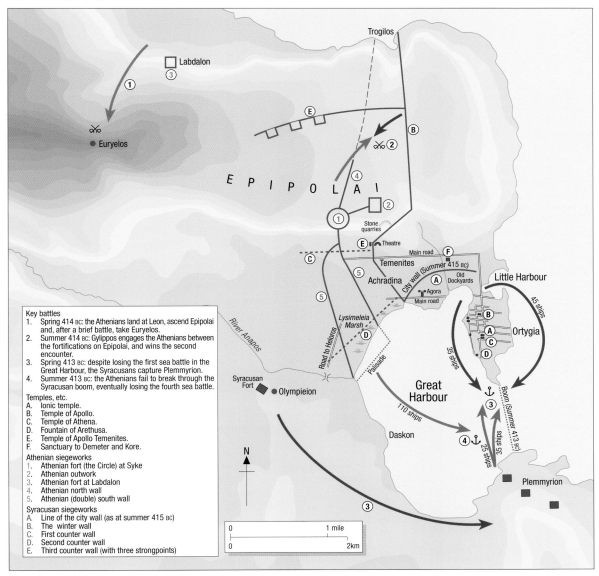

Key battles
1. Spring 414 BC: the Athenians land at Leon, ascend Epipolai and, after a brief battle, take Euryelos.
2. Summer 414 BC: Gylippos engages the Athenians between the fortifications on Epipolai, and wins the second encounter.
3. Spring 413 BC: despite losing the first sea battle in the Great Harbour, the Syracusans capture Plemmyrion.
4. Summer 413 BC: the Athenians fail to break through the Syracusan boom, eventually losing the fourth sea battle.

Temples, etc.
A. Ionic temple.
B. Temple of Apollo.
C. Temple of Athena.
D. Fountain of Arethusa.
E. Temple of Apollo Temenites.
F. Sanctuary to Demeter and Kore.

Athenian siegeworks
1. Athenian fort (the Circle) at Syke
2. Athenian outwork
3. Athenian fort at Labdalon
4. Athenian north wall
5. Athenian (double) south wall

Syracusan siegeworks
A. Line of the city wall (as at summer 415 BC)
B. The winter wall
C. First counter wall
D. Second counter wall
E. Third counter wall (with three strongpoints)

Still, the investment was almost complete. Lack of timber prevented the immediate completion of their north wall, that running across Epipolai to the sea at Trogilos, but this was only a matter of time, or so the Athenians believed. Nikias had also taken Plemmyrion, the waterless headland forming the southern side of the entrance to the Great Harbour, and the run of Athenian triumphs had won them the support not only of many of the Sikels, but also of the Etruscans, who sent three 50-oared ships to their aid. Meanwhile the Syracusans were beginning to discuss surrender not only among themselves but with Nikias (6.103.3), and sacked their *stratêgoi*, including Hermokrates, electing three new ones in their place. After the two attempts to build counter-walls from their 'winter wall' had been defeated, they were delivered a further crippling blow when the Athenian fleet sailed into their harbour. Syracuse was now blockaded by sea.

RIGHT
Thapsos, looking north-north-east from Castello Eurialo. Seen here like an extended, crooked finger, the peninsula is almost an island, since its only connection with the mainland is a sandy isthmus 2.5km long and 100m wide at one point. (Fields-Carré Collection)

BELOW, RIGHT
Thapsos' northern shore, looking south-west from the prehistoric settlement. The peninsula lies only 10km north of Syracuse, and it was under this leeward shore that the Athenian fleet laid up for a time before finally moving into the Great Harbour. (Fields-Carré Collection)

HELP ARRIVES

It was at this point, however, that Nikias became overconfident, ignoring the one distant cloud in the otherwise bright Athenian sky. As will be recalled, the Syracusans had sent representatives to the Peloponnese asking for assistance and Corinth, as the mother-city of Syracuse, had pressed Sparta to act. Initially Corinth and Sparta dispatched only four triremes (two Corinthian and two Spartan) and a handful of troops, but leading them was a determined and resourceful Spartan warrior, Gylippos son of Kleandridas (6.93.2).

Although news had reached Nikias of the Spartan's arrival in Italy some time before, he had taken no action against such a contemptible force. Meanwhile, Gylippos and the Corinthian admiral Pythen were making their way to Sicily under the impression that the Athenians had already completed their investment of Syracuse, but at Lokroi (Locri) on the toe of Italy they learned the truth and set out to save the city, sailing to Himera on the north coast to avoid the Athenian fleet. When Nikias learned of their arrival at Lokroi he decided to dispatch four ships to intercept them, but the response came too late. The Himeraians joined Gylippos and provided arms for his sailors. More help came from Selinous and Gela and from the Sikels, who switched sides because of the death of their pro-Athenian ruler and the persuasive zeal of Gylippos. And so with a handful of *neodamôdeis* serving as marines, the armed sailors of four triremes, and an odd assortment of allies, Gylippos set out for Syracuse.

Additional support was already on the way to the beleaguered city in the shape of 13 triremes manned by the Corinthians and their allies. One of them, under Gongylos of Corinth, slipped through the blockade and arrived at the

ABOVE
The northern escarpment of Epipolai, looking north-east from Castello Eurialo towards Targia. It was on these cliffs at a spot Thucydides (6.97.5) calls Labdalon that the Athenians erected a fort, where they stored their supplies, equipment and war chest. (Fields-Carré Collection)

LEFT
Epipolai, looking north-west from Porto Grande. The optimum location from which to control and command a siege operation, it was somewhere near the clump of trees on the southern escarpment that the Athenians had their fort known as the Circle. (Fields-Carré Collection)

ARRIVAL OF THE SPARTAN WARRIOR (pp. 62–63)

When a long-haired man with a distinctive cloak entered Syracuse in the summer of 414 BC, people knew the long-awaited Spartan mission to Sicily had arrived. To the amusement of the enemy, Gylippos (1) was the only Spartan, albeit a *mothax*, in the entire relief column. Apart from an array of allies, the rest consisted of, in Thucydides' words, 'an army of new citizens (*neodamôdeis*) and helots' (7.58.3), some 400 of them if they were the armed crew of two Spartan triremes (6.104.1, 7.1.3, 5). When further reinforcements arrived the following year, they again included 'picked men from among the *neodamôdeis* and helots, 600 hoplites in all, under the command of Ekkritos, a full Spartan citizen' (7.19.3). It appears that our otherwise unsung Ekkritos was the single solitary Spartiate sent to Syracuse by Sparta.

In this scene we see Gylippos enter the city on foot, followed by his helot shield-bearer (2). The closed Corinthian helmet has been replaced by the *pilos* helmet (3), a simple bronze cap distinguished by its conical shape and narrow rim. Spartan swords (4) had become shorter and straighter; so much so that by the Peloponnesian War they were exceedingly short, virtually dirks or even daggers – allegedly because Spartans fought at such close quarters.

At some point, certainly by 412 BC and maybe as early as 422 BC, Sparta began to use the letter Λ (*lambda*) for Lakedaimonians as a state shield device. A fragment of the Athenian poet Eupolis, possibly dealing with Kleon's Thracian campaign, suggests the Spartans applied this letter on their shields. His last known comedy was staged in 412 BC, and he died the following year

'in the Hellespont', in all probability at the naval engagement off Kynossema. The letter was painted (and repainted) onto the bronze face of the shield in the uniform crimson colour, and it soon became, like the hairstyle and cloak of the Spartan warrior, a weapon of terror. Eupolis, in the aforesaid fragment, makes light of Kleon's fear of the 'dreaded *lambdas*' (fr. 359 Kock).

The hair continues to be dressed (and oiled) in four locks falling to the front, two on either shoulder, and four to the back and the upper lip continues to be shaved, but the beard is generally longer than before. Originally a garment typically worn by labourers to allow free movement of the right arm, the Spartans have adopted the *exomis* (5) for warfare. This tunic is two-sleeved, but the right-hand sleeve can be let down to leave the right shoulder and arm free to handle weapons in combat providing, of course, the warrior lacked body armour.

Over his linen corselet (*linothôrax*, 6) Gylippos wears the trademark Spartan cloak (7). Called a *tribôn*, it is habitually described as being 'mean' (*phaulos*), that is to say, thin as opposed to short. Spartan boys under training had to wear the same cloak in summer and winter in order to become accustomed to the cold. Self-denial is the keynote to the Spartan lifestyle, and warriors would visually emphasize their toughness by making use of a single woollen cloak, rain or shine, allowed to wear thin and never washed. Like the tunic, it is dyed crimson. No less than a uniform and no less of a distinctly Spartan trait, especially abroad, is the walking stick (8) (*bakteriâ*) with a T-shaped crosspiece at the top, which allows the traveller to lean on it when stationary.

The southern escarpment of Epipolai, looking north from Punta Caderini. What Thucydides (7.53.2) calls the Lysimeleia marsh once stretched from the centre to the far left of this photo. It was here that the two arms of the Athenian double wall touched the shore. (Fields-Carré Collection)

city even before Gylippos reached it over land. Gongylos appeared in the nick of time, for the Syracusans were about to surrender. He persuaded them not to hold the decisive assembly, reporting that more ships were on the way and that Gylippos had been sent by the Spartans to organize the defence. Gylippos himself came onto the Epipolai from the west through Euryelos, the same route the Athenians had taken, marched around the unfinished north wall, and entered the city.

Once in the city the dynamic Gylippos put fresh heart into the beleaguered Syracusans. They started the construction of four strongpoints and a third counter-wall, which was to run north of the Circle parallel to the northern escarpment of Epipolai so as to block the route of the Athenian wall of circumvallation as it crept north towards Trogilos. Nikias understood what was about to unfold and accepted battle, Gylippos having daily led out the Syracusan army and drawn it up in front of the lines, that is, between the completed portion of the third counter-wall and the northern end of the completed section of the Athenian wall. As there was little or no room between the fortifications for the Syracusan cavalry and javelineers to operate freely, the Syracusans were defeated.

Calling the soldiers together, Gylippos confessed the fault was not theirs but his, and said he would lead them against the enemy for a second time. They needed to bear in mind that their equipment was as good as the enemy's, and that 'it would be an intolerable thing if Peloponnesians and Dorians could not fall certain of defeating and driving out of the country these Ionians and islanders and rabble of all sorts' (7.5.4). The hostility between Dorian and Ionian is a constant theme in Thucydides, who conceptualizes a war-worn Greek world divided between a Dorian alliance, headed by Sparta, and an essentially Ionian one, led by Athens. Anyhow, tribal conflict aside, in the ensuing second battle, with room to manoeuvre on the right, the Syracusan cavalry and javelineers routed the enemy left, whereupon the whole Athenian army collapsed and fled back to the safety of the Circle. Unwittingly helped by the Athenians, who had placed piles of stone along the intended line of their own wall, the Syracusans were now able to carry their counter-wall past the end of the Athenian north wall. This was the decisive moment of the campaign.

It was now obvious that the Athenians could not invest Syracuse. As if to stress this point, Gylippos also captured the Athenian fort at Labdalon and annihilated its garrison. Likewise, the Athenians were unable to prevent the arrival of the remaining 12 ships of the Corinthians and their allies under the command of the Corinthian Erasinides. The crews of these ships, some 2,400 men, were immediately put to work, enabling the Syracusans to complete their counter-wall across Epipolai. With these positive developments the Syracusans' confidence increased dramatically, so much so that they began to train their naval crews with the intention of challenging the invaders ship for ship at sea.

Nikias was unable to formulate a real response. He gathered many troops and most of the equipment in three forts he had constructed at Plemmyrion. It was something of a retreat to safety, which demoralized the men. Obtaining what little fresh water and fuel were available was difficult, as the Syracusans were superior in horsemen. As Thucydides points out, with 'the occupation of Plemmyrion, the Syracusans had stationed one-third of their cavalry at the village of Olympieion, to prevent the Athenians coming out and plundering the countryside' (7.4.6). The relocation to Plemmyrion also dangerously divided Athenian forces.

NIKIAS WRITES HOME

With summer turning to autumn, Nikias now saw the danger of the besiegers being besieged, at least on land, and wrote to Athens to ask permission to retire or, failing that, for more troops to be sent. In the letter, which Thucydides purports to quote verbatim, Nikias first summarizes the Athenian reverses on land and then sets forth the current state of affairs, namely the growing threat at sea. The Athenian triremes had deteriorated because they could not be hauled ashore and dried out in case the enemy attacked, and because they had to maintain the blockade. For the Syracusans, on the other hand, 'it is easier for them to dry their ships, since they are not maintaining a blockade' (7.12.5). Since a dry ship was both faster and less apt to rot than a waterlogged one, crews regularly pulled their triremes out of the water when they were not in use.

The state of the Athenian crews had also deteriorated because of the attentions of the Syracusan cavalry when they went out to forage or plunder, while slaves and foreign sailors were deserting. Some oarsmen had even 'bought Hykkaric slaves and then persuaded the *triêrarchoi* to take these slaves aboard instead of themselves, thus ruining the efficiency of the fleet' (7.13.2). Nikias then explains why he feels he is unable to lift the siege and leave Syracuse before it is all too late, saying that he knows 'the Athenian character from experience: you like to be told pleasant news, but if things do not turn out in the way you have been led to expect, then you blame your informants afterwards. I therefore thought it safer to let you know the truth' (7.14.3). This statement is perhaps the most damning indictment of the Athenian system of direct democracy, at least in wartime.

Instead of relieving a commander with a defeatist attitude, the Athenian assembly chose to increase the stakes and voted for a second lavish expedition. This was a bold (or foolhardy) move, because the war with Sparta was about to start again and the Athenians could ill afford to squander men and *matériel*. Nevertheless, they promoted two men on the spot as interim support and appointed two new *stratêgoi*, Demosthenes, the hero of Pylos, and Eurymedon, who was making a comeback to Sicily. The latter set out at once with 120 talents and ten triremes, and sailed straight to Sicily,

TOP

Capo Santa Panagia, looking east from Targia. The rocky inlet just to the west of the cape, Caladi Santa Panagia, is ancient Trogilos. The Athenian north wall was meant to reach this point, thereby completing their circumvallation from sea to sea. (Fields-Carré Collection)

CENTRE

Having won the first sea-battle in the Great Harbour, the Athenians towed away 11 Syracusan wrecks and set up 'a trophy upon the islet in front of Plemmyrion' (Thucydides 7.23.4). Two of three such islets are visible here. (Fields-Carré Collection)

BOTTOM

Plemmyrion, looking north-east from Punta Spinazza. It was on this headland forming the southern side of the harbour entrance that Nikias erected three forts-cum-depots. These were to be seized by Gylippos using a combination of land and naval forces. (Fields-Carré Collection)

even though it was 'about the time of the winter solstice' (7.16.2). He then returned to liaise at Corcyra with Demosthenes who meanwhile was preparing to spend the winter assembling the main reinforcements.

THE TIDE TURNS

As the Athenians prepared to strengthen their position in Sicily, Gylippos' success also convinced the Spartans to dispatch additional forces to the island. They planned to send three contingents. One was made up of 600 *neodamôdeis* and helots commanded by the Spartiate, Ekkritos, and a second, consisting of 300 Boiotians under their own *stratêgoi*, would depart from Cape Tainaron, the central and most southerly of the three promontories of the southern Peloponnese; they would sail together across the open sea. A third force of 700 hoplites made up of Corinthians, Sikyonians and Arcadian mercenaries would sail west through the Gulf of Corinth and past the Athenian base at Naupaktos, protected by a convoy of 25 Corinthian triremes.

Back in Syracuse, meanwhile, Gylippos decided that it was imperative to finish off Nikias' command before the arrival of Demosthenes. The first stage had to be the seizure of the forts at Plemmyrion. Through the suave eloquence of Hermokrates, he persuaded the Syracusans to fight a sea-battle on the following day, after he had brought the land forces secretly during the night around to Plemmyrion. The Syracusans launched their attack early in the morning with 80 triremes, which were met by 60 Athenian ships. After an initial success, the Syracusans were defeated owing to their lack of experience. But the Athenian garrison had gone down to the shore to watch the naval engagement, which had been anticipated by Gylippos. Leading the attack by land from the Olympieion, he swiftly captured the three forts, which contained a wealth of naval equipment, and established control over Plemmyrion.

This defeat on land forced the Athenians to crowd into an inadequate camp in unhealthy, marshy ground on the west side of the Great Harbour. But the strategic cost of the capture of the headland was even greater, as the Syracusans now held both sides of the harbour. The Athenians could no longer bring in supplies, and 'the loss of Plemmyrion brought bewilderment and discouragement to the army' (7.24.3).

Lysimeleia marsh, looking east from Molo San Antonio. At the time of the siege the marsh extended from the southern cliffs of Epipolai southwards to the Anapos river. After the loss of Plemmyrion, this insalubrious location became the main Athenian camp. (Fields-Carré Collection)

Somewhat desperate now, Nikias tried to exploit his naval superiority by closing with the Syracusans in the Great Harbour, but he was thwarted in his attempts. The Syracusans declined to give battle and instead kept their triremes in front of what Thucydides calls the 'old dockyards' (7.25.5). Situated in the north-east bay of the harbour, these dockyards were protected by a palisade constructed from massive stakes that had been driven into the seabed. In an effort to breach this obstacle, the Athenians fitted out a large merchant ship with wooden towers and a protective screen along its sides. In the small hours, they brought this floating bastion up to the stockade, and under its protection small boats rowed up to the stakes, 'fastened ropes round them, and dragged them up with windlasses, or broke them off short, or dived under the water and sawed through them' (7.25.6). But it was all to no avail; as soon as the Athenians withdrew, the stakes were immediately replaced.

The second stage of Gylippos' plan was to defeat Nikias' navy. To overcome their vulnerability on the sea, the Syracusans triremes were redesigned for fighting in the narrow waters of the Great Harbour: they reduced the length of the bows and reinforced the cat-heads with stay-beams, an innovation borrowed from the mother-city Corinth (7.36.2). This strengthening of their prows now meant that the Syracusans could ram head on, while the Athenians, in the confined waters of the harbour, would not be able to execute their favourite tactics of the *periplous* or the *diekplous*. Basically, the ram of the Syracusan trireme would, after a bow-to-bow collision, slide along the ram of its Athenian opponent and its cat-head, the stout beam structure projecting laterally just aft of the prow supporting the outrigger; it would then smash into and, having been strengthened, tear into the cat-head of the more lightly constructed Athenian trireme, taking the attached outrigger with it. It is important to understand that the outrigger was attached to the gunwale on each side of the trireme, and on it were fixed the oar pins of the top-level oarsmen.

Gylippos planned a joint attack by land and sea to put added pressure on the Athenians. The land forces threatened the Athenian double wall from opposite sides, from the city and from the Olympieion, while 80 Syracusan triremes prepared to take on 75 Athenian ships. The first day's fighting proved inclusive, and on the following day there was no engagement, so

The 5th-century ship sheds, looking west-south-west on Via Agatocle. Once part of the old dockyards, these covered slipways allowed the Syracusans to drag their triremes out of the water and weather for repair and drying. (Fields-Carré Collection)

The bow of *Olympias* showing one of the box-like *epótides* or cat-heads, which protect the outriggers. This was the structure the Syracusans reinforced with stay-beams, thereby allowing their triremes to ram the Athenians head on, bow to bow. (Fields-Carré Collection)

Nikias used the lull to prepare for the next attack. The Athenians had sunk a palisade into the sand beneath the sea some distance offshore to serve as an enclosed harbour. To make it easier to defend vessels pulling out of battle, Nikias anchored a line of merchant ships, about 60m apart, in front of this palisade. Each ship carried a crane armed with heavy iron weights in the shape of a dolphin. The crane could drop the 'dolphin' onto a pursuing enemy vessel and 'sink' or disable it.

On the third day the Syracusans attacked, and again the battle became a long skirmish, which lasted until the Syracusans withdrew for rest and lunch on the beach, where merchants were setting up a food market for the hungry crews. The Athenians likewise headed for shore, believing that the fighting was done for the day. As the men were eating, however, the Syracusans suddenly launched another assault, and the tired, hungry and stunned Athenians barely succeeded in putting their ships to sea.

The Syracusans met the Athenians with the head-on charge, as well as a few new tricks. They had loaded their decks with javelineers whose missiles disabled many Athenian oarsmen. Skiffs carrying additional javelineers slipped in under the oar banks of the Athenian triremes, allowing them to incapacitate even more oarsmen. The disruption caused to the working of the oar crew by an intruding missile can be imagined. These unorthodox tactics and the modifications of their prows proved decisive, and the Syracusans won their first naval victory over the invaders, who were able to escape disaster only by fleeing to safety behind the merchantmen and the palisade. Two reckless Syracusan triremes that pursued too aggressively were destroyed by the 'dolphins'. Seven Athenian triremes were 'sunk' and a large number were damaged. The Syracusans dominated the Great Harbour and set up a trophy.

THE LAST VENTURE

Just as things were looking bleak for Nikias and his men, however, Demosthenes and the second expedition swept into the Great Harbour, with 73 triremes carrying almost 5,000 hoplites, and a large number of lightly armed troops 'both from Greece and from outside' (7.42.1). With his characteristic clarity and boldness, Demosthenes recommended an attack to destroy the Syracusan third counter-wall and seize Epipolai, for without the heights no assault on the city could prevail. But the siege machines he tried to use were set on fire as they were dragged forward, presumably from the Circle, and everywhere his attacks were beaten off.

Realizing that by day it would be impossible to avoid detection, Demosthenes opted to make the second attempt by night. In the silvery light of a bright moon the Athenians reached the top of the escarpment without being observed. They captured the strongpoint at Euryelos, though they were unable to prevent most of the garrison escaping to the other three strongpoints on Epipolai. Despite the alarm having been raised, Demosthenes

maintained the momentum of his attack and pressed his troops forward to secure the counter-wall. Having reached their objective without meeting any resistance, the Athenians at once set about tearing it down.

However, Gylippos ordered a counter-attack with the troops holding the other strongpoints, and in the confusion of the night fighting the Athenians became disjointed and dispersed. Worse still, unable to distinguish friend from foe, some of them started fighting one another. According to Thucydides it was the war cry (*paean*), simultaneously raised both by their Dorian allies and by their Dorian enemies, which caused so much confusion and did as much harm as anything else. 'Thus', says Thucydides, 'when the Argives and Corcyraeans and other Dorian elements in the army started singing their *paean* they produced as much panic among the Athenians as the enemy did' (7.44.6). Failure to distinguish friendly from hostile Doric accents meant the Athenians were unable to locate their allies and perceived their enemies to be on all sides.[2] The resulting disaster was decisive. This defeat brought an end to the Athenian aims of taking Syracuse and conquering Sicily; they were replaced by the solitary aim of survival.

THE LUNACY OF NIKIAS

The army was clearly in a bad way, and Demosthenes believed they should not delay any longer, but evacuate the remnants of the expeditionary force while they still had a fleet. Demosthenes was backed by Eurymedon, but Nikias held the opposite view. They should not withdraw without the consent of the Athenian assembly; otherwise their political opponents would turn public opinion against them and indict them. Moreover, once back in Athens their disgruntled veterans would turn against them and convince the fickle assembly that it was the *stratêgoi* who were to blame for the failure. They would complain 'that their *stratêgoi* had been bribed to betray them and return. For

Epipolai, looking east from Castello Eurialo. Though deceptively flat, the topside of the plateau is mainly exposed, bare limestone with scrub oak, ankle-breaking terrain at the best of times. It was across this surface the Athenians made their night attack. (Fields-Carré Collection)

2 Since the hoplites of both sides purchased their own equipment and still displayed individual shield blazons, visual recognition was practically impossible. State shield devices were just being introduced but would not become universal until the next century.

NIGHT ATTACK ON EPIPOLAI (pp. 72–73)

Demosthenes saw that the third Syracusan counter-wall was the key to the whole situation. He therefore planned to seize and destroy it, take control of Epipolai, and then push on with the siege. Demosthenes ordered his men to take five days' rations, and assembled all the stonemasons, carpenters and archers, and everything else they might require, to complete their circumvallation. Then, at what Thucydides calls 'the first sleep' (7.43.2), he himself, with Eurymedon and the bulk of the army, set off, leaving Nikias in the lines. Epipolai is over 100m up, exposed limestone with scrub oak, sheer on its three sides except at its apex near Euryelos in the west, where it is steep but climbable. The barren plateau topside measures some 4.5km west to east and just fewer than 3km at the waist. It was going to be a long and difficult haul.

That afternoon the soldiers made the necessary preparations for the forthcoming operation, including the eating of a hot meal. Having roasted and milled their barley, the Athenian hoplites would have taken their flour and kneaded it up with a little oil and wine, using a square of sheepskin as a kneading-trough, to produce a simple form of unleavened bread (Thucydides 3.49.3, Hermippos fr. 57 Kock). The fresh dough would then be twisted around a stick and baked in the hot ashes of their camp fires. Despite Xenophon's claim (*Kyropaideia* 1.2.11) that when he was truly famished even barley-bread tasted sweet, it was usually helped down with a little local wine and a wedge of cheese,

with onions, garlic, olives, anchovies and thyme-flavoured salt as likely accompaniments (Thucydides 4.26.5, Aristophanes *Acharnians* 550-551, 1099, *Knights* 599, *Peace* 368).

That night, having ascended by the hill of Euryelus unobserved by the Syracusan guards, the Athenians captured the fort there from the enemy, putting them to flight. Those fleeing managed to raise the alarm in the three camps on the heights, which were manned by Syracusans and their allies, including the Corinthians. These advanced against the Athenians, but were routed by them after a sharp resistance. Meanwhile other Athenians had taken the third counter-wall of the Syracusans.

The Syracusans and their allies, together with Gylippos and the troops under his command, advanced to halt the Athenians from their outworks. The Athenians (1) had begun to lose order in their advance, and came up against the Boiotians (2), whose brave stand put the Athenians to flight. Although there was a bright moon the fighting degenerated into utter confusion, with one man unable to tell friend from foe in the uncertainties of a night engagement. 'Thus,' as Thucydides says, 'after being once thrown into disorder, they ended by coming into collision with each other in many parts of the field, friends with friends, and citizens with citizens, and not only terrified one another, but even came to blows and could only be parted with difficulty' (7.44.7).

his own part, therefore, knowing the Athenian character as he did, rather than be put to death on a disgraceful charge and by an unjust verdict of the Athenians, he preferred to take his chance and, if it must be, to meet his own death himself at the hands of the enemy' (7.48.4). In other words, he would sooner meet his death as a soldier than be executed at home as a criminal.

However, Athenian dismay at the arrival of more enemy troops at last brought Nikias round to accepting the necessity of withdrawal. But it was not to be. A lunar eclipse caused the superstitious Nikias to delay the expedition's departure for 'the thrice nine days recommended by the *manteis*' (7.50.4). Deserters informed the Syracusans that the Athenians were planning to sail home but were delayed by the lunar eclipse. The Syracusans thus became more determined than ever not to relax their pressure and decided to force the enemy to fight again in the confined space of the Great Harbour. They began to train their crews for a decisive battle.

Attacks were made by sea as well as land, with 76 Syracusan ships engaging 86 Athenian. The result was another Athenian defeat. Eurymedon had been killed attempting to outflank the enemy's left by executing the *periplous*, and his death was the signal for the rout of the entire Athenian fleet (7.52.2). There had been some local Athenian successes, helped by the Etruscans, but the Syracusans had won a decisive victory at sea. With virtually complete command of the Great Harbour, the Syracusans prepared themselves for what would be the fourth and final sea-battle.

The Athenians first abandoned the Circle and built a cross-wall linking the two arms of the double wall as close to the shore as convenient, allowing sufficient room for their equipment and the sick. This they could defend, but with the rest of their soldiers and sailors they manned every vessel they had, seaworthy or not. They then attempted to try and break through the improvised boom of merchantmen thrown across the harbour entrance by the Syracusans.

The Athenians, with 110 ships, made straight for the entrance, and the impetus of their charge carried them through the Syracusans' screen of ships to the line of anchored vessels that they were guarding. But as they were trying to break the boom and clear a passage to the open sea, the rest of the Syracusan fleet bore down on them and the fighting spread over the full extent of the harbour. Because there were nearly 200 ships crammed in such a confined space, and despite the best efforts of the helmsmen, there were

The Great Harbour, looking south-west on Passegio Adorno towards Daskon. It may appear as a vast watery expanse, but on the fateful day of the fourth and final sea-battle some 200 ships were crammed into this 640 hectare-area. (Fields-Carré Collection)

few opportunities to ram, backing water and executing the *diekplous* being impossible. Instead, accidental collisions between friend and foe alike were numerous. Thucydides now takes up the story:

> All the time that one ship was bearing down upon another, javelins, arrows, and stones were shot or hurled on to it without cessation by the men on the decks; and once the ships met, the marines fought hand to hand, each trying to board the enemy. Because of the narrowness of the space, it often happened that a ship was ramming and being rammed at the same time, and that two, or sometimes more, ships found themselves jammed against one, so that the helmsmen had to think of defence on one side and attack on the other and, instead of being able to give their attention to one point at a time, had to deal with many different things in all directions; and the great din of all these crashing together was not only frightening in itself, but also made it impossible to hear orders given by the boatswains. And indeed, in the ordinary course of duty and in the present excitement of battle, plenty of instructions were given and plenty of shouting was done by the boatswains on either side. To the Athenians they cried out, urging them to force a passage and now, if ever, to seize resolutely upon the chance of a safe return to their country; and to the Syracusans and their allies the cry was that it would be a glorious thing to prevent the enemy from escaping and for each man to bring honour to his own country by winning the victory. (7.70.5–7)

After a day-long struggle the Athenians finally broke. Those who were not taken afloat ran for the camp as they came ashore.

One Athenian kept his head at this terrible moment. Demosthenes saw that the Athenians still had 60 viable triremes to fewer than 50 for the enemy, and proposed that they collect their forces and try another breakout from the harbour at daybreak. It seemed a feasible plan, as the Syracusans would not have expected another such attempt. But it was too late, however, for the morale of the men had collapsed entirely. They refused the orders to board the ships again and insisted on endeavouring to escape by land.

The Athenian retreat from Syracuse

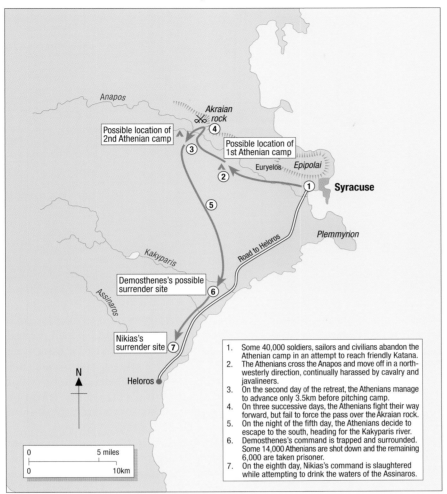

1. Some 40,000 soldiers, sailors and civilians abandon the Athenian camp in an attempt to reach friendly Katana.
2. The Athenians cross the Anapos and move off in a north-westerly direction, continually harassed by cavalry and javalineers.
3. On the second day of the retreat, the Athenians manage to advance only 3.5km before pitching camp.
4. On three successive days, the Athenians fight their way forward, but fail to force the pass over the Akraian rock.
5. On the night of the fifth day, the Athenians decide to escape to the south, heading for the Kakyparis river.
6. Demosthenes's command is trapped and surrounded. Some 14,000 Athenians are shot down and the remaining 6,000 are taken prisoner.
7. On the eighth day, Nikias's command is slaughtered while attempting to drink the waters of the Assinaros.

TOTAL ANNIHILATION

Abandoning their sick and wounded comrades, 40,000 Athenians and their allies started the overland trek to Katana, a place loyal to Athens that could furnish a friendly welcome and much needed supplies. The plan was to follow the Anapos upstream, meet amiable Sikels somewhere in the highlands, and turn northwards towards Katana. The Syracusans were anxious to prevent such a withdrawal, fearing that the Athenian army would be re-equipped and sent against them a second time. Gylippos sent out detachments to make roadblocks and to harass the retreat as much as possible. Nikias led the van while Demosthenes commanded the rearguard, but they made little progress. On the night of the fifth day they gave up, and decided to march in the opposite direction – something the Syracusans had not expected them to do. But it did not improve the situation for the Athenians.

On the sixth day of the retreat the two columns became separated under the constant harrying of the Syracusan cavalry and javelineers. Demosthenes' command was surrounded and, after being assailed by missiles throughout the day and suffering heavy casualties, the surviving 6,000 threw down their

arms. Plutarch alleges (*Nikias* 27.2) that Demosthenes tried to take his own life but was prevented by his captors. Meanwhile, Nikias and his men pressed on, only to have the pursuit catch up with them by the next day. Informing Nikias that Demosthenes and his men had surrendered, the Syracusans offered the same terms, but he refused to believe them. Instead, on behalf of Athens, he offered to reimburse Syracuse the total cost of the war, one Athenian to be hostage for each talent of silver, if his command was allowed to go. In reply the Syracusans launched a full-scale attack.

The next day, the eighth, Nikias' starved and thirsty command continued the retreat, making its way to the Assinaros under a barrage of missiles from all sides. But on reaching the river, Athenian discipline finally cracked. Soon a milling mass was down in the riverbed, while from above the Syracusans picked them off as they drank from the river, 'all muddy as it was and stained with blood' (7.84.4). Nikias gave himself up to Gylippos, and only then did the Spartan generalissimo order an end to the killing, the few survivors being rounded up and taken prisoner.

Nikias and Demosthenes were executed without trial, against Gylippos' wishes: he wanted to take them back to Sparta, particularly Demosthenes, 'Sparta's greatest enemy because of the campaign at Pylos' (7.86.3). The 7,000 captives were sent to the stone quarries, where all perished of exposure, starvation or disease after eight months of incarceration there, save for the few who were lucky enough to be sold into slavery or those who, according to legend, were able to recite verses by Euripides from memory (Plutarch *Nikias* 29.2).

This was Athens' greatest reverse and a turning point in the Peloponnesian War. Thucydides, emphasizing the foolhardy ambition so typical of imperial democracy, says 'the Athenians were beaten at all areas and altogether; all they suffered was great; they were annihilated, as the saying goes, with a total annihilation, their fleet, their army – everything was annihilated, and few out of many returned home' (7.87.6). The expedition had been lost in its entirety, every ship, every man. To most Greeks it seemed Athens' imperial days were all but few in number.

The Anapos river, looking west from Via Elorina bridge. Retreating from Syracuse, the Athenians followed the river upstream. They slugged their way as far as what Thucydides calls the 'Akraian rock' (7.78.5), modern Monte Climiti (406m) seen rising in the distance, before being checked. (Fields-Carré Collection)

THE CAMPAIGN IN RETROSPECT

The visually brilliant departure of the Athenian armada is described by Thucydides (6.30–32.2) with all the appropriate drama and detail. The entire city, both citizens and foreigners, went down to the Peiraieus to see the grand spectacle. Prayers were offered up, and libations poured from cups of gold and silver. The magnificently equipped fleet then put to sea, ships racing each other as far as Aegina. Thucydides did not witness this 'regatta', but he no doubt spoke to some who did. He also drew on a long and rich tradition of poetic narrative, and his vivid picture was doubtless coloured by his knowledge that few of those who set out on that glorious day ever came home. His scene reminds us, suitably, of Pindar's picture of the departure of the Argonauts, whose captain Iason, on the ship's stern, 'took a golden bowl in his hands, and called on Zeus the lightning-wielder, the father of the Ouranidai' (*Pythian* 4.193-194). But then, once they had crossed the Adriatic, came the rejection at Rhegion, which evidently depressed morale, as did the discovery that the financial promises made by the Egestaians were next to worthless. Unlike Iason, who, with his travelling companions, was to enjoy a spectacular adventure overseas, the Athenians had bitten off more than they could chew.

If, with all the benefits that hindsight affords us, we are looking for failings that doomed the Athenian expedition then we have five. First, the neutrality of people who had been expected to behave as allies. Their nominal ally Egesta proved a broken reed and, apart from some of the Sikels, only Katana gave them any real support. Second, Athenian inferiority in the cavalry arm, which then only put in one appearance, albeit none too successful (7.51.2), after its first showing (6.98.1). Third, the failure to follow up the initial surprise, above all by wintering at Katana. As Syracuse was the main objective it was nonsensical to waste the summer on operations in the west of the island, and land near the city, win a battle and sail away 'because it was now winter' (6.71.2). All this did was galvanize resistance. Fourth, the recall of the brilliant Alcibiades, which was bad for morale though he had not

THE FINAL SEA-BATTLE (pp. 80–81)

The Syracusans, determined to secure not merely the salvation of their city but the complete destruction of the invaders, set out to shut them in the Great Harbour. Accordingly, they anchored a line of merchantmen and other hulks across the harbour entrance, bridging them over with boards, and connecting them with iron chains. Part of the fleet had been detailed to guard this boom, while the rest created a ring around the harbour, ready to charge the Athenians from all points of the compass when the time was ripe. In the meantime, the hoplites occupied all the places along the shoreline where ships could put in.

Since the only feasible escape route was by sea, the Athenians (1) opted to try to break through this improvised boom. Having manned every ship able to float and boarded everyone likely to be of service as a marine, the Athenians geared themselves to fight a land battle at sea. To meet the enemy's tactic of ramming head-to-head with strengthened cat-heads, they forged 'iron-hands', or grappling irons (2), which were designed to seize an attacking trireme and prevent it from backing away after having driven into the prow of an Athenian trireme. By making fast with grappling irons, which were on short lengths of chain to prevent the grappling ropes from being cut immediately, the marines (3) could then board the enemy ships. Deserters, however, warned the enemy of these measures, and so the Syracusans stretched hides across the prows and upper sections of their ships (4) to make the grappling irons slip off.

The Assinaros river, looking east from the Calabernardo–Marina d'Avola road. It was somewhere along the course of this river that Nikias' command finally met its end. The Syracusans stood on the south bank and smothered the parched Athenians with missile fire. (Fields-Carré Collection)

done anything brilliant yet. All the same, with him and his companions gone, the armada had lost not only its boldest and most enterprising officers, but those most passionately devoted to the expedition. Despite a recent tendency to belittle his achievements, Thucydides, who probably knew the man, says that his military conduct 'was excellent' (6.15.4), and possibly thought that even the expedition might have succeeded had he been left in command. Perhaps with proper reflection common sense would have informed the Athenians that, as the main advocate for the expedition, Alcibiades was most unlikely to jeopardize either the venture or his own quest for glory by flouting public religious susceptibility through cavalier sacrilegious pranks. Fifth, the failure to recall the ailing and demoralized Nikias when he asked for this but to send reinforcement. It is an approved maxim in war that one should never reinforce failure.

These five failings all belong to what we would call the strategic level of war. But at the tactical level the Athenian *stratêgoi*, Nikias particularly, were responsible for one major mistake, namely the failure to vigorously prosecute the siege of Syracuse itself.

Greek siegecraft

For most of the classical period fortification walls do not have a place in that central moment of Greek warfare, the clash of opposing phalanxes. The ethic of hoplite warfare and the practical restrictions imposed by the heavy panoply meant the hoplite was ill equipped to deal with the difficulties of cracking fortified positions. The equation between hoplite status and citizenship also made the rate of casualties a significant political consideration, and the relatively small citizen populations of many of the *poleis* magnified this factor. Since the hazardous adventure of a direct assault generally imposed the greatest number of losses, there was a tendency to shun such operations unless unavoidable.

What the citizens of a *polis* had to fear most from their fellow Greeks was reduction by starvation or their betrayal to the enemy from within. Though Diodoros (12.28.3) credits Perikles with the use of battering rams (*krious*) and tortoises (*chelônas*) against Samos in 440 BC, Thucydides says (1.117.3) the city held out for eight months and then capitulated, which suggests

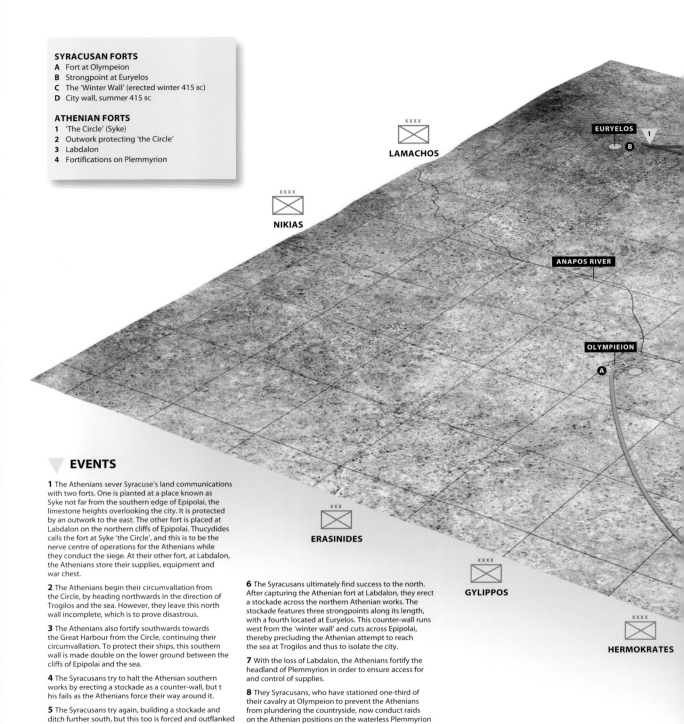

SYRACUSAN FORTS
A Fort at Olympeion
B Strongpoint at Euryelos
C The 'Winter Wall' (erected winter 415 BC)
D City wall, summer 415 BC

ATHENIAN FORTS
1 'The Circle' (Syke)
2 Outwork protecting 'the Circle'
3 Labdalon
4 Fortifications on Plemmyrion

LAMACHOS

EURYELOS

NIKIAS

ANAPOS RIVER

OLYMPIEION

ERASINIDES

GYLIPPOS

HERMOKRATES

▼ EVENTS

1 The Athenians sever Syracuse's land communications with two forts. One is planted at a place known as Syke not far from the southern edge of Epipolai, the limestone heights overlooking the city. It is protected by an outwork to the east. The other fort is placed at Labdalon on the northern cliffs of Epipolai. Thucydides calls the fort at Syke 'the Circle', and this is to be the nerve centre of operations for the Athenians while they conduct the siege. At their other fort, at Labdalon, the Athenians store their supplies, equipment and war chest.

2 The Athenians begin their circumvallation from the Circle, by heading northwards in the direction of Trogilos and the sea. However, they leave this north wall incomplete, which is to prove disastrous.

3 The Athenians also fortify southwards towards the Great Harbour from the Circle, continuing their circumvallation. To protect their ships, this southern wall is made double on the lower ground between the cliffs of Epipolai and the sea.

4 The Syracusans try to halt the Athenian southern works by erecting a stockade as a counter-wall, but t his fails as the Athenians force their way around it.

5 The Syracusans try again, building a stockade and ditch further south, but this too is forced and outflanked by the Athenians.

6 The Syracusans ultimately find success to the north. After capturing the Athenian fort at Labdalon, they erect a stockade across the northern Athenian works. The stockade features three strongpoints along its length, with a fourth located at Euryelos. This counter-wall runs west from the 'winter wall' and cuts across Epipolai, thereby precluding the Athenian attempt to reach the sea at Trogilos and thus to isolate the city.

7 With the loss of Labdalon, the Athenians fortify the headland of Plemmyrion in order to ensure access for and control of supplies.

8 They Syracusans, who have stationed one-third of their cavalry at Olympeion to prevent the Athenians from plundering the countryside, now conduct raids on the Athenian positions on the waterless Plemmyrion headland.

THE BATTLE FOR CONTROL OF EPIPOLAI

Epipolai was the key to control of the city of Syracuse, dominating the ground below and safeguarding the access of food and supplies. The battle to control the heights saw fortifications and counter-works erected by both sides. Ultimately, the Athenian failure to cut the city off to the north allowed the Syracusans to secure the heights and push the Athenians back to Plemmyrion.

LABDALON

3

TROGILOS

6

EPIPOLAI

2

1

2

3

4

TEMENITES

C

D

LITTLE HARBOUR

5

LYSIMELEIA MARSH

ORTYGIA

DASKON

GREAT HARBOUR

N

7

PLEMMYRION

4

8

4

4

85

Latomia del Paradiso, taken from within the quarry. In the search for compacted limestone, this huge and staggering piece of work was dug into the rock to an extraordinary depth. Once the quarry was exhausted, the cavities were used as a prison. (Fields-Carré Collection)

that it was reduced by blockade, by starvation or the fear of starvation, rather than by direct assault. Plataia, after ingenious attacks that seem to have been the acme of contemporary Greek siegecraft was, in the end, left to fall to the long-drawn pressure of starvation after two years of close-drawn circumvallation (2.75–78, 3.52.1–2). Actually this siege highlights the real weakness of Greek siegecraft, and is a clear indication of the difficulties that still stood in the way of capturing a city during the Peloponnesian War even with the latest techniques available.

The Athenians had some reputation for siegecraft (1.102.2), but Poteidaia held out against them for nearly three years and then surrendered only on terms, and that too although it was important for Athenian prestige to bring the siege to an end as quickly and decisively as possible (2.70.1–3). When Mytilene revolted against Athens in 428 BC the city could not be taken until the beginning of starvation led to its surrender the following summer. In fact capitulation only came about when the mass of the citizens were armed and were able to get their way against the more determined oligarchs who had been responsible for bringing about the rebellion in the first place (3.27–28). Similarly, some form of *coup de main*, helped by local treachery, captured the Long Walls at Megara (4.66–68).

For the Athenians the prolonged encirclement and starvation of the trapped populace may have been the keys to victory, but mounting a formal siege was a ruinously expensive undertaking. The reduction of Samos had cost over 1,400 talents (Fornara 113), while that of Poteidaia was an even greater financial drain, costing no less than 2,000 talents or two-fifths of the expendable reserves currently available to Athens (2.70.2). But it was the operations against Mytilene that strained Athenian fiscal resources almost to breaking point. The Athenians, needing money for the siege, decided on a desperate solution and 'raised among themselves for the first time a property-tax of two-hundred talents' (3.19.1).

The Athenians themselves had deployed 'machines' (*mêchanai*) against Samos (Plutarch *Perikles* 27.7) and Poteidaia (2.58.1), and Nikias from his ships at Minoa (3.51.3). This unqualified term is entirely indefinite, but almost certainly included the scaling-ladder, battering ram, tortoise and shed, although not the catapult, which had yet to be invented. It is somewhat ironic, therefore, that the only 'machines' mentioned in Thucydides' account of the siege of Syracuse are those Nikias burned to delay an attack on the Circle (6.102.2), and those Demosthenes attempts to use on the Syracusan third counter-wall, which were burned by the enemy before being dragged or put into place (7.43.1). Yet if circumvallation was the best way to take Syracuse, Nikias bungled it. He failed to complete the investment of the city by delaying the construction of a single line of circumvallation before the other building projects, that is, a double wall from the Circle down to the Great Harbour and fortifying Plemmyrion.

AFTERMATH

The Sicilian venture had probably claimed at least, from Athens alone, 3,000 hoplites and 9,000 *thêtes* as well as thousands of *metoikoi*. The Athenians probably now had 9,000 hoplites of all ages, perhaps 11,000 *thêtes*, and 3,000 *metoikoi*, fewer than half of the number available when the Peloponnesian War started. They had lost 216 triremes, of which 160 were Athenian; only about a hundred, not all of which were seaworthy, remained. Of the 6,000 expendable talents available in 431 BC fewer than 500 now remained in the treasury. For Syracusans, however, the booty was immense. They were able to build a splendid treasury at the oracular sanctuary of Delphi, 'from the great Athenian disaster' (Pausanias 10.11.4), to store a tenth of the proceeds of this war, the standard tithe dedicated to Apollo.

Meanwhile in Athens, when the news sank in, the citizens 'turned against the public speakers who had been in favour of the expedition, as though they themselves had not voted for it' (8.1.1). The Athenians eventually came to their senses and appointed a board of older men, one of whom was the tragedian Sophokles of Kolonos, to take a preliminary look at issues as they arose. This was normally the job of the *boulê*, and, although that body was not abolished and despite the inclusion of a man like Sophokles, who had been associated and worked with Perikles, the very nature of the new council had an oligarchic ring. This is, indeed, the first hint of the reaction against democracy that was to bring about its overthrow the following year.

WAR AT SEA

In the summer of 412 BC, Hermokrates fulfilled the fears supposedly expressed by various speakers in Athens three years previously (6.6.2, 10.1, 18.1), by arriving from the west to assist the Peloponnesians with a fleet of 20 Syracusan and two Selinountine triremes (8.26.1). The crippling failure of the expedition to Sicily meant that the enemies of Athens were at last encouraged to cross the Aegean, and not only challenge its domination of the seaboard of western Anatolia but also threaten its vital lifeline to the Black Sea.

Athens was dependent on maritime imports, especially grain and flax from the Black Sea region, and so its navy was responsible for the protection of sea-borne commerce, particularly those passing through the Hellespont (Dardanelles). However, hitherto Sparta had been unable to match the might of the Athenian navy, only having the capability to dispatch a motley fleet of amateurs and allies to stir up the occasional revolt within their maritime empire.

The aftermath in the Aegean, 413–411 BC

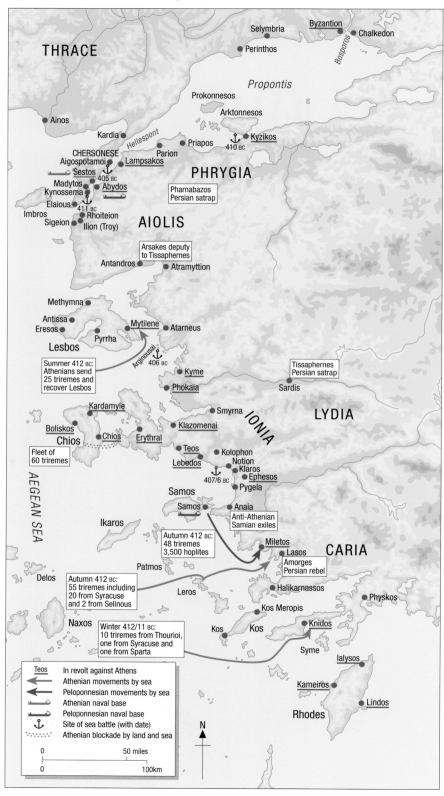

THRACE

Selymbria
Byzantion
Chalkedon
Perinthos

Propontis

Prokonnesos

Arktonnesos

Ainos

Kardia
Hellespont
Priapos
Kyzikos
410 BC

CHERSONESE
Aigospotamoi
Parion
Lampsakos
Sestos
405 BC
PHRYGIA
Madytos
Abydos
Kynossema
Elaious
411 BC
Imbros
Rhoiteion
Sigeion
Ilion (Troy)
AIOLIS

Pharnabazos
Persian satrap

Arsakes deputy
to Tissaphernes

Antandros
Atramyttion

Methymna

Antissa
Eresos
Mytilene
Atarneus
Pyrrha
Arginousai
406 BC
Lesbos

Summer 412 BC:
Athenians send
25 triremes and
recover Lesbos

Kyme

Phokaia

Tissaphernes
Persian satrap

Smyrna
Sardis

Kardamyle
LYDIA

Boliskos
Chios
Klazomenai
IONIA
Chios
Erythrai

Fleet of
60 triremes

Teos
Kolophon
Lebedos
Notion
Klaros
407/6 BC
Ephesos
Pygela

Samos
Samos
Anaia
Anti-Athenian
Samian exiles

AEGEAN SEA
Ikaros

Autumn 412 BC:
48 triremes
3,500 hoplites

Miletos
Lasos
CARIA
Amorges
Persian rebel

Patmos
Delos
Leros
Halikarnassos
Physkos

Autumn 412 BC:
55 triremes including
20 from Syracuse
and 2 from Selinous

Kos Meropis

Kos
Kos
Knidos

Naxos
Syme

Winter 412/11 BC:
10 triremes from Thourioi,
one from Syracuse and
one from Sparta

Ialysos

Kameiros

Lindos

Rhodes

Teos — In revolt against Athens
→ Athenian movements by sea
← Peloponnesian movements by sea
⚓ Athenian naval base
Peloponnesian naval base
⚓ Site of sea battle (with date)
Athenian blockade by land and sea

N

0   50 miles
0   100km

Latomia del Paradiso, looking north-west on Via Ettore Romagnoli, the largest of many deep quarries excavated into the cliffs of Epipolai. Now beautifully covered with citrus and pomegranates, it was here that some 7,000 Athenians were incarcerated and left to rot. (Fields-Carré Collection)

At the start Sparta sent a fleet to blockade the geopolitical choke point of the Hellespont. Despite this stratagem however, King Agis, who was holding the fort at Dekeleia, reckoned it was a waste of time attempting to sever Athens' supply lines when he could still see the Black Sea grain fleet putting into the Peiraieus. The alternative, of course, was to engage Athens on the high seas, but in doing so Sparta was to suffer misfortune on a number of occasions.

Kynossema (autumn 411 BC) was a moral victory for the Athenians who, lacking their former confidence, had been afraid of the Peloponnesian fleet with its Syracusan allies, 'but now they got rid of their feelings of inferiority and ceased to believe that the enemy was worth anything at sea' (8.106.2). Soon after Kynossema, there was near to Abydos a hard-fought engagement, which turned in favour of the Athenians with the timely arrival of Alcibiades and 18 triremes. Once again, the Athenians commanded the narrow waters of the Hellespont. Both sides now asked their home governments for more men and ships, as they prepared for the next conflict over mastery of the straits.

Kyzikos (spring 410 BC) was a scrambling fight along the southern shore of the Propontis (Sea of Marmara), but by the end of the day the main Peloponnesian fleet and its Spartan admiral Mindaros had been eliminated, and again this was chiefly due to Alcibiades. Thucydides has now ceased to be our main source and his place is taken by Xenophon, who talks of a dispatch, intercepted, from the remnant Spartans to their home government: 'Ships sunk, Mindaros slain, men starving. Don't know what to do' (*Hellenika* 1.1.23). By the conclusion of Kyzikos the Spartans had lost between 135 and 155 triremes within the space of a few months. Kyzikos gave Athens command of the high seas for the better part of the next three years.

As matters now stood, however, the Persians could build the Spartans another fleet, even a bigger one. Worse still, the Athenians remained short of funds, with many sources of imperial revenue still in Spartan hands, so the enemy could outbid them for the services of experienced oarsmen from the empire. Eventually the Athenians were obliged to use inexperienced men as oarsmen, including peasant farmers, aristocrats who normally served in the cavalry corps, and even slaves, who, according to Aristophanes, were offered freedom and Athenian citizenship for their service 'in a single sea-battle' (*Frogs* 693, cf. Fornara 164A).

The 'single sea-battle' was that off the Arginousai islands (summer 406 BC), east of Lesbos. There the Peloponnesian triremes, 'with their more skilful crews, were drawn up in a single line abeam so as to be able to execute the *diekplous* and the *periplous*' (Xenophon *Hellenika* 1.6.31), while the Athenians, lacking their former confidence and inferior in seamanship, formed a double line, one behind the other, so as not to give the Peloponnesians the chance to execute these manoeuvres. The Peloponnesians were heavily defeated and Kallikratidas, the Spartan admiral, fell overboard and drowned. Money could not make up for an indifferent commander.

THE FALL OF ATHENS

Sparta ultimately gained the upper hand. Its formidable admiral Lysandros, having been restored to supreme command despite the illegality of appointing the same man to the position twice, resoundingly defeated the Athenians at Aigospotamoi, dead across the Hellespont from Lampsakos and only a few kilometres from Alcibiades' castle (summer 405 BC). Lysandros employed stealth and superior tactical skill to capture – on the open beach – almost the entire Athenian fleet. Many Athenian sailors were slaughtered, while those who survived Lysandros had killed in cold blood; the bodies were left unburied as an awful warning. The navy on which Athens depended for its security and its food supply was all but annihilated. Only nine or twelve of 180 triremes survived the débâcle, and, with their treasury empty, the Athenians could not afford to build another fleet.

The following spring Lysandros was able to strangle the Athenians into submission, his thundering victory having effectively left their grain transports at the mercy of the Peloponnesian fleet. Brought to their knees, the Athenians were forced to swear an oath 'to follow the Spartans by land and sea, wherever they might lead' (Xenophon *Hellenika* 2.2.20). Their cherished democracy was then replaced by a pro-Spartan oligarchic junta backed by a Spartan garrison, a murderous puppet government who deservedly acquired the nickname of Thirty Tyrants. There was no longer an Athenian assembly.

In the letter he wrote to the assembly back home while his command slowly rotted outside Syracuse, Nikias complained bitterly of the decline of the crews and the acute shortage of experienced personnel to man the fleet. Athens resorted to hiring mercenary crews, yet with crucial financial backing from Persia the Spartans were often able to outbid the Athenian recruiting officers and thus produce a navy that was not only as large but also as technically competent as the Athenian. Likewise, Persian gold enabled them to float new fleets and hire new crews when battles were lost. It was, therefore, by sea, paradoxically for the normally landlubbing Spartans, that the thrice-nine-year war with Athens had been decided.

CITIZEN SOPHOKLES

In the summer of 430 BC, following the winter in which Perikles had delivered his Funeral Speech (2.34–46), a devastating plague struck Athens. In the wake of the physical suffering caused by the disease, which Thucydides reports (2.52–54) with clinical interest and was probably typhus, came the beginnings of a moral and social revolution. What the plague was to Athens for a few years, the Peloponnesian War was to Greece as a whole for a generation.

Thucydides describes it like a disease, worsening by stages and ending in the collapse of the cultural ideas that he ascribes to Perikles. Nowhere does he make this view clearer than when he describes (3.82–83) the incredibly bloody internal struggle that took place between the democrats and the oligarchs on the island of Corcyra in 427 BC.

The physical upheaval in Greece during the war, which is implicit in Thucydides, becomes explicit in the greatest of Athenian dramas of the time. Sophokles' *Oedipus Tyrannus*, produced in 429 BC, portrays a masterful ruler who enters the scene as a renowned riddle solver, ferociously intellectual, flushed with confidence from previous success, optimistic, seemingly in firm control of his world but, significantly enough, faced with an inscrutable plague in his city. At the end of the play he is blinded, powerless and an outcast, comprehending too late the nature of great forces of which he was not the master.

The Greek *poleis* and the factions within them were being drawn, through their quest for *holos*, into the never-ending cycle of *hubris* and *nemesis*, which they themselves had seen in the undoing of the Persians. Sophokles, pious and traditional by nature, seems bothered in *Oedipus Tyrannus* not by the blindness or irrationality of fate but by the blindness and inherent arrogance of the 'man is the measure' philosophy. The pride of the 'hymn to man' in the *Antigone* (lines 332–68), written in the 440s, had turned to deep anxiety by the 420s.

Sophokles himself was a model citizen. When he was 14 he had led a chorus of other Athenian boys in a poem to celebrate the defeat of the Persians at Salamis. When he reached maturity his voice was too weak for him to become an actor, but he did compose over 100 plays – of which seven survive – and won at least 20 victories, 18 of them at the Greater Dionysia. He was thus markedly the most successful of the three great Athenian tragedians. The son of an aristocrat who had made money in the arms industry, Sophokles himself served as one of the *stratêgoi* during the revolt of Samos in 440 BC. Some say that the *Antigone*, in which the rights of the state are given full weight against those of the individual, earned him this position. Others suggest that his disgust at the exposure of the enemies' corpses, having first been crucified and then beaten to death on the orders of the arch-imperialist Perikles, might have led him to write this tragedy.

THE FATE OF ALCIBIADES

According to Plutarch, Alcibiades' golden shield was 'not emblazoned with any ancestral device' (*Alcibiades* 16.2) but with an outrageously flamboyant blazon – a thunderbolt-wielding Eros, which advertised his fabled aggressive sexuality. His choice of emblem had caused a scandal in Athens because it was felt it expressed *hubris*. It was his choice of bedfellow that was to scandalize Sparta.

By the late summer of 412 BC Alcibiades had sought refuge with the Persians after Agis, one of Sparta's two kings, learned that he had been sleeping with his wife. Once in the realm of the Great King, whose empire dwarfed that of Athens, Alcibiades offered to negotiate for the Athenians, but part of the deal involved their acceptance of a watered-down version of their maverick constitution. Athens was a democracy, and exported this radical (and idiosyncratic) form of popular government to its subject-allies. Its successful annexation of the Aegean islands and coastal regions of Anatolia deprived the Great King of revenue and encouraged rebellion amongst his Greek subjects.

The grave stele of Lisas the Tegean, one of Sparta's allies serving in the garrison of the fort at Dekeleia. His dress and equipment are patently modelled on Spartan lines, as Lisas wears an *exomis* tunic and *pilos* helmet. (Reproduced from *BCH* 4, 1880, plate VII)

Yet the shattering defeat of the Athenian navy at Syracuse meant the backbone of radical democracy had been removed. Worse still, 'the subjects of Athens were all ready to revolt' (8.2.2) and the Spartans, with Persian gold, started to build a fleet, a fleet that would be very far from being just the usual puny flotilla that Sparta alone could or would muster. In the meantime, Athens itself was ripe for an oligarchic *coup d'état*, the brainchild of Alcibiades. Once again the mercurial Alcibiades was meddling in local politics, on this occasion advocating to the Persians that the Athenians would sacrifice their cherished democratic rights if Persia switched its support from Sparta to Athens. Thucydides, who probably knew him personally, suggests that his advice to the Persians was designed not only to injure the Spartans, who had ordered his execution, but also to engineer his recall to Athens. He was convinced that 'the dreadful democracy that had exiled him' (8.47.2) would never pardon him, and consequently that the establishment of an oligarchy was the essential precondition for his return to Athens.

However, the following year Alcibiades seems to have shifted his ground, and once again preferred his native city's cause. The attempt to secure Persian support floundered but the plot had gathered its own momentum by now. Supporters of oligarchy had always existed amongst the Athenians, grumblers like the Old Oligarch implacably opposed to the aims and methods of democracy, or 'bad government' (*kakonomia*); but what was different about 411 BC was that many Athenians – and not only the oligarchs – had begun to consider a change of regime in an attempt to help the war effort. Yet while the hoplites of Athens, disillusioned and angry, were initially in favour of this oligarchic counter-revolution, the navy, manned by the poorest and most democratically minded Athenians, remained resolutely opposed.

The fleet's main Aegean base was the island of Samos, and it was here that the representatives of the new regime at Athens came to try to persuade the fleet to sail back to its home port, the Peiraieus. Alcibiades, who just happened to be on Samos, realized that such a departure would cost Athens its control of the Hellespont, and persuaded the fleet's commanders, Thrasyboulos and Thrasyllos, both of whom were long-time associates of his, to remain at their Samos base and thus establish what was virtually a democracy in exile. This, his sober contemporary Thucydides (8.86.3) comments acerbically, was the first great act of service that Alcibiades had done for his motherland.

In Athens meanwhile, the Four Hundred, as the savagely repressive oligarchic regime became known, held power through acts of terror and assassination. However, this revolutionary council could never win over the *thêtes* in the eastern Aegean fleet. Radical democrats to a man, the *thêtes*, quite naturally, refused to surrender their political rights. Eventually, the Four Hundred were formally deposed and power was handed over to the Five Thousand, citizens who could provide themselves with the panoply of a hoplite or serve in the cavalry corps. What this short-lived regime amounted to is controversial, even more so because Thucydides voices an opinion at this juncture, perhaps giving us an insight into his personal views on democracy. He praises the Five Thousand, saying that:

During the first period of this new regime the Athenians appear to have had a better government than ever before, at least in my time. There was a reasonable and moderate blending of the few and the many, and it was this, in the first place, that made it possible for the polis to recover from the bad state into which its affairs had fallen. (8.97.2)

It is almost impossible, at times, to see what he actually means, and he was, perhaps, too intelligent for his own and our good; however, as he says, 'so ended the oligarchy and the *stasis*' (8.98.4). Yet there was one very good reason why this so-called moderate constitution was destined to fail. Athens' rise to superpower status had been achieved by the sweat of its citizen-oarsmen, common men accustomed to full political rights. The continuing survival of Athens, therefore, lay with the *thêtes* at Samos. Another result of the victory at Kyzikos may have been the restoration of full democracy at Athens.

By the summer of 407 BC Athenian fortunes in the Hellespontine region had spectacularly recovered and Alcibiades was welcomed home in triumph and given full command of the eastern Aegean fleet. Within six months he had been rejected by the Athenians. The occasion was the failure of his personal helmsman, Antiochus, who at Notion, in Alcibiades' absence, had accepted battle against strict instructions (late 407 BC or early 406 BC). Alcibiades was not condemned in court, he was not even formally accused; but he was not elected *stratêgos* for the following year. He left the fleet and sought a world elsewhere. Taking only one ship, he sailed away to the Hellespont, where he had the foresight to acquire a heavily fortified estate. There, amongst the Thracians, he recruited a private army and embarked on the life of a brigand chief, successfully doing so until 404 BC when he was hunted down by hired killers sent by his enemies, who could have been Spartan, Persian, Thracian or Athenian.

In Aristophanes' *Frogs*, produced within a year of Alcibiades' second fall from favour, Euripides asks what the Athenians thought about Alcibiades, Dionysos, the patron god of drama, replies: 'they love him, hate him, and want to have him back' (line 1425). Deprived of his services as a result of Notion, the Athenians, who between 410 BC and 406 BC had looked like winning the Peloponnesian War after all, could now hardly fail to lose it. Just before the catastrophe at Aigospotamoi in the high summer of 405 BC, we glimpse the brilliance of Alcibiades for the last time, warning the Athenian *stratêgoi* against recklessly beaching their ships where they could be exposed to attack by the enemy (Xenophon *Hellenika* 2.1.25–26). His help was scornfully rejected and, having been reminded that he was no longer in command, he rode off.

Castello Maniace (1239), looking north from the harbour entrance, Syracuse. It was built by Frederick II, but was erroneously named after the renowned Byzantine general, George Maniakes. The Swabian castle is square with round corner towers, a plan and spatial form derived from Byzanto-Muslim architecture. (Fields-Carré Collection)

BIBLIOGRAPHY AND FURTHER READING

Bagnall, N. *The Peloponnesian War: Athens, Sparta and the Struggle for Greece* (London: Pimlico, 2004)

Cartledge, P.A. *The Spartans: An Epic History* (London: Channel 4 Books, 2002)

Cerchiai, L., Jannelli, L. and Longo, F. *Greek Cities of Magna Graecia and Sicily* (Verona: Arsenale Editrice, 2004)

Everson, T. *Warfare in Ancient Greece: Arms and Armour from the Heroes of Homer to Alexander the Great* (Stroud: Sutton, 2004)

Forde, S. *The Ambition to Rule: Alcibiades and the Politics of Imperialism in Thucydides* (Ithaca, NY: Cornell University Press, 1989)

Fields, N. *Ancient Greek Fortifications, 500–300 BC* (Oxford: Osprey Fortress 40, 2006)

Fields, N. *Ancient Greek Warship, 500–322 BC* (Oxford: Osprey New Vanguard 132, 2007)

Hanson, V. D. *The Western Way of War: Infantry Battle in Classical Greece* (London: Hodder & Stoughton, 1989)

Hanson, V.D. (ed.) *Hoplites: The Classical Greek Battle Experience* (London: Routledge, 1991, 1993)

Kagan, D. *The Peace of Nicias and the Sicilian Expedition* (Ithaca, NY: Cornell University Press, 1981)

Kagan, D. *Fall of the Athenian Empire* (Ithaca, NY: Cornell University Press, 1987)

Kagan, D. *The Peloponnesian War: Athens and Sparta in Savage Conflict 431–404 BC* (London: Harper Collins, 2003)

Krentz, P. 'Fighting by the rules: the invention of the hoplite *agon*', *Hesperia 71*, pp. 23–39 (2002)

Lazenby, J. F. *The Peloponnesian War: A Military Study* (London: Routledge, 2004)

Liebeschütz, J. H. W. G. 'Thucydides and the Sicilian expedition', *Historia 17*, pp. 289–306 (1968)

Meiggs, R. *The Athenian Empire* (Oxford: Clarendon Press, 1972)

Morrison, J. S. and Coates, J. F. *The Athenian Trireme: The History and Reconstruction of an Ancient Greek Warship* (Cambridge: Cambridge University, 1986, 2nd edition, 2000)

Rutter, N. K. *Thucydides VI and VII: A Companion* (Bristol: Bristol Classical Press, 1989, 2002)

Sage, M. M. *Warfare in Ancient Greece: A Sourcebook* (London: Routledge, 1996)

Sekunda, N. V. *Greek Hoplite 480–323 BC* (Oxford: Osprey Warrior 27, 2000)

Shaw, J. T. (ed.) *The Trireme Project. Operational Experience 1987-90. Lessons Learnt* (Oxford: Oxbow Monograph 31, 1993)

de Ste. Croix, G. E. M. *The Origins of the Peloponnesian War* (Oxford: Clarendon Press, 1972)

Strassler, R. B. (ed.) *The Landmark Thucydides: A Comprehensive Guide to the Peloponnesian War* (New York: Touchstone, 1996, 1998)

Van Wees, H. *Greek Warfare: Myths and Realities* (London: Duckworth, 2004)

Westlake, H. D. *Individuals in Thucydides* (Cambridge: Cambridge University Press, 1968)

A note on Thucydides

Thucydides (*c.* 455–400 BC), son of Oloros, was an Athenian who wrote an unfinished account of the Peloponnesian War. He himself in 424 BC served as one of the ten elected *stratêgoi*, and he was subsequently exiled at the end of that year for his failure to save Amphipolis from the shrewd Spartan commander Brasidas. During his exile in Thrace, where his family had connections and property (his father's name is probably Thracian and princely), he compiled his history of the war. His exile, he claims (5.26.5), gave him opportunities for appreciating the point of view of each of the combatants.

This unfinished masterpiece, *History of the Peloponnesian War*, is our most important single source for the dispatch and fortunes of the Sicilian expedition mounted by Athens. Thucydides obviously was an eyewitness to many of the events and personalities he describes, or at least was able to gain information from reliable sources. Our problem in seeing the war through his eyes (until 411 BC, at any rate, when his account breaks off amid the events of that year) is certainly not one of having to eliminate crude bias in favour of his own side and against the enemy, but the more subtle difficulty of escaping from his densely written narrative, which does not furnish us with alternative accounts.

It is therefore sometimes easy to mistake his overall interpretation of events and their significance as an authoritative narrative. The speeches, of which there are 141 presented both in direct and indirect discourse, are an especial problem. Thucydides says (1.22.1) he wrote what he could remember of the speeches that he heard, but also wrote what seems likely to have been said on an occasion; therefore, one can easily imagine the problems this presents.

INDEX